POWER TO US ALL

POWER TO US ALL

CONSTITUTION
OR
SOCIAL CONTRACT?

GEORGE WOODCOCK

HARBOUR PUBLISHING

Copyright © 1992 by George Woodcock

HARBOUR PUBLISHING
P.O. Box 219, Madeira Park, BC Canada V0N 2H0

Cover design by David Lester
Printed and bound in Canada

The assistance of the Canada Council and the Cultural Services Branch, Ministry of Municipal Affairs, Recreation and Culture, Government of British Columbia are gratefully acknowledged.

Canadian Cataloguing in Publication Data

Woodcock, George, 1912–
    Power to us all

    ISBN 1-55017-073-2

    1. Nationalism—Canada.   2. Federal-provincial relations—Canada.*   4. Canada—Politics and government. 5. Canada—Social conditions.   I. Title.
JL31.W65 1992   320.471   C92-091515-9

CONTENTS

Permutations of Power: An Introductory Essay

I

"I VOTED AGAINST THE CONSTITUTION because it was a constitution!" said the great French political philosopher, Pierre Joseph Proudhon during the French Revolution of 1848 when he was asked why he had been among the tiny minority of the National Assembly voting against proposals for a constitution. His attitude was not based merely on his libertarian view that society should be allowed to develop its institutions empirically and organically, rather than by formal fiat. He also pointed out that in a constitution which divided powers, the tendency would always be for the executive, the most rigid, centralist and power-oriented branch of government, to take control. His point was well taken, and history has given it justification in the centuries since the American states adopted their own pioneer constitution. Louis Napoleon Bonaparte, the president of France elected under the constitution that Proudhon rejected, made himself first a dictator and then an emperor. And with only brief intervals, the president of the United States has represented all that is reactionary and overbearing in American life and in the American attitude towards the world in general. I need hardly expand on the offences against basic human rights that have taken place under the apparently benign constitutions of the Soviet Union in the past, or the People's Republic of China in the present.

II

IN HIS RECENT BOOK, *The Betrayal of Canada*, Mel Hurtig remarks that "Our quarrelsome preoccupation with the constitution is looked upon with disdain and despair by people both inside and outside Canada"; this did not prevent him from entering into the fray with his own constitutional proposals for protecting Canada from the raptorial practices of the transnational corporations. And it is tempting to stand aside at times and consider that some countries—notably Britain, which lives by a formless body of custom and precedent, common law and statutes—have done without formal constitutions; and they have prospered more than many nations with formally intricate and virtually unobserved constitutions, negated, as in all the Communist countries, by the seizure and enjoyment of power by the executives.

Yet, while it may be salutary for us to remember the instances where people still live reasonably well by custom and law and without enclosing themselves in the straitjacket of a constitution, we have to bear in mind the general inclination of Canadians during the past decade of the millennium, which suggests that they are intent on making some kind of political garment within which their notable variety can be contained. Given this curious inclination towards self-restraint, the problem becomes that of making the least restrictive jacket in political terms, one offering the maximum diffusion of authority at the top, and the maximum popular participation at the bottom. In its actual ways of living, no country is more naturally pluralist than Canada. This follows from its traditional social and geographical variations. As the historian David Jay Bercuson remarked during the earlier constitutional fever of 1981, "Canada is a country of regions, distinguished by geographical setting, economic role, history, culture, and even by different political ambitions for the same Canada to which they all belong."

To bring these creative diversities together without inhibiting them should surely be the principal task of any document setting out political relations in Canada. It must recognize that a country so vast, where the provinces are often larger than nation-states in the Old World (and larger than most member states of the United Nations), the local loyalty is primary; if that does not exist, the wider loyalty to such a vague and impalpable concept as Canada will not flourish.

The splendour of Canada lies not merely in its superb (if sometimes monotonously grand) terrain, but also in the way geography conspired with history to develop a whole series of local traditions that gain by their mingling, yet must retain their separateness for their mingling to be meaningful. The ferociously independent Greek cities of the archaic age mingled to produce the splendid civilization without borders that we remember as Hellas. Just as their splendid totality depended on the individual intensity of the Athenian and Ionian and Corinthian visions, so the Canadian vision will acquire a splendid totality through people whose loyalty is local first. Without that close identity with habitat and local traditions, the greater loyalty to Canada as the home of all these cultures will have no vitality. Our variousness is in fact the very cement that holds us together, and any constitution worth creating for this land, so badly exploited and so often foolishly governed in the past, must be based on the great Canadian virtue of diversity in unity.

Thus, the *main* aim of the constitutional exercise should be the protection of the successful diversity that makes Canada unique, and offers the world one example of how to escape from the crumbling walls of the obsolescent nation-state. Unfortunately, the euphoric talk of the quest for "Canadian unity," so characteristic of the autocratic era of Pierre Elliott Trudeau, is still to be heard in the discussions of constitutional reform. I received the other day a call from a central Canadian magazine asking my views on the prospect of achieving "national unity," and I remarked impatiently that what interested me was not the achievement of "national unity," but the accomplishment of "creative anti-national disunity." I spoke mostly without jest, for I believe that the neo-Jacobin goal of the "nation one and indivisible" that Trudeau tried to foist on us is an entirely reactionary one, looking back to the political errors of 1789 in Paris; whereas the act of confederation, fostered in 1865–67 in small colonial towns like Charlottetown and Québec, established in Canada the model for true federalism—a model that has lain almost as somnolent as a bewitched princess for a century and more. Nonetheless, it offered to anyone who could penetrate the dark wood—and still offers—the kind of polity that could be a refuge for freedom in the age of collapsing nation-states and empires through which we are living. Properly developed, it could offer a defence against the transcontinental commercial condottiere of the late twentieth century.

"At the moment," Mel Hurtig declares in *The Betrayal of Canada*, "Canada is disintegrating." Perhaps the nation-state that Sir John A. Macdonald and his successors tried to superimpose on the country with their disastrous "National Policies" is indeed disintegrating; this would be all to the good. It is good for Canada that the Québecois sustain their independent vision, that westerners refuse to abandon their discontent with the continuing pretensions of the Toronto–Ottawa–Montréal economic and political axis, that the Maritime communities, clinging like Old World limpets to the shores of the New World, remember the splendid sea-going economy that post-confederation policies destroyed; that Newfoundlanders still sometimes sing "Come near at your peril, Canadian wolf." Perhaps it is as well, also, to remember the exhortation of Amor de Cosmos, the British Columbian patriot, that "I would not object to a little revolution now and again in British Columbia, if we were treated unfairly, for I am one of those who believe that political hatreds attest the vitality of the state." It is only by feeling our differences strongly, by budging reluctantly but in the end with conviction, that we shall ever achieve, through a true and lasting consensus, that deep unity of the diverse which the Swiss, to give only one example, have long ago attained.

III

AS THIS BOOK PROCEEDS, I shall be examining the various aspects of the relations between Canadians, both as individuals and as communities, and I shall be stressing the advantage we have over other countries: a true head start in escaping from the prison of the nation-state, through the confederal nature of our origins.

Yet confederation is actually the third of the alternatives offered to Canada and its peoples today, and the scant attention and understanding it has received is one of my main reasons for writing of it now.

We have heard plenty about the separatist solution, about even the possibility of Canada breaking up entirely if Québec departs from the confederation, and I shall return more extensively to such matters in discussing the notion of "distinct societies." But it is the so-called federalist solution that has received most attention outside Québec through being advanced by a series of central governments, and by most of the provincial and territorial governments, without very much attention to alternatives.

In Canadian political debate, "federal" generally means nothing like a true confederation of regions and communities, but our present outworn system of a central government and a cluster of provincial governments, elected separately; it is not in fact even a genuine federal system, in which the central council is chosen by the local assemblies and their members are given delegate, not plenary powers. As interpreted in Canada, "federalism" has actually embraced many gradations of attitude. Sir John A. Macdonald, a confessed believer in legislative union, supported the confederation of Canada in 1867 only as the last chance of bringing and keeping British North America together. He was always trying with his National Policy to turn Canada into a nineteenth-century nation-state, and the provincial leaders—supported by the Privy Council in London, then our ultimate court of appeal—strove to preserve and expand their autonomy by constantly reinterpreting the British North America Act (BNA) in a confederalist direction. Pierre Trudeau, a true confederationist in his youth, later adopted Jacobinical notions and became an advocate of what he and his kind have called "strong central government," meaning an Ottawa-based autocracy.

In fact, ever since Canada's birth in 1867, the political history of the country has been dominated by a struggle between provincial politicians and Ottawa cabinets over the division of powers specified—or unanticipated and therefore unspecified—in the BNA. What both sides in this perennial contest have shared is a disinclination to extend power downward to people organizing themselves locally, by devising such traditional populist devices as the initiative, the referendum and the power of recall. The most obscene example of the reluctance of Canadian establishments to develop power occurred when federal and provincial leaders closeted themselves, with all the secrecy of a Papal conclave, at Meech Lake in the fortunately unsuccessful attempt to concoct a constitutional accord. That proposal would have preserved their respective areas of power without opening any avenues to direct democracy, to a deeper involvement of the people. It was an irony of epic proportions that all this unworthy intrigue should have been frustrated in the end by one powerless man, Elijah Harper, making day after day—as he held up his symbolic eagle's feather—his speech of a single eloquent word: "No!"

I shall be dealing later with the questions of Québec distinctiveness and Native sovereignty, both of which I strongly support in my own way, and wish to see extended. But I support them within the context of a genuine confederation, and an eventual flexible social contract establishing a basis for new arrangements between groups and individuals. I believe this could be Canada's great contribution to a global reassessment of concepts of national sovereignty, a reassessment that is appropriate to our traditions as an inevitably pluralist society.

IV

THE INTENT OF THIS BOOK is not historical. More than a decade ago, in *Confederation Betrayed* (1981), I traced in detail the history of the confederal idea in Canada, and the way it was undermined by successive power-oriented political leaders. But it is necessary to refer to the origins of Canada as we know them, so as to remind readers that the first aim of the confederating colonies when they came together was not to create a legislative union; New Brunswick and Nova Scotia were much too distrustful of the Canadas for that. It was to make the historical and geographical and cultural elements of the separate colonies workable in a confederation.

There have been two views among historians of what happened when the Dominion of Canada came into being. One is that Canada's establishment occurred as a fiat of the imperial power, but this is true only to the extent that the British Colonial Office encouraged an existing trend among colonial politicians, and the British Parliament — anxious at this time to lighten imperial responsibilities — eventually passed the BNA, bringing the colonies together as the provinces of a new country. But the BNA itself only came into being because of the initiative of the colonies, resulting from meetings of their political leaders at Charlottetown in

September 1864, and the following month in Québec. They met as representatives of sovereign polities, and this is clearly stated in the opening words of the Preamble to the original North America Act, drafted by Macdonald himself in Westminster in 1867.

A federation with confederal possibilities was actually established, and during the succeeding decades it settled into shape as the various provinces sought to define and strengthen their roles in government; sometimes, as in the cases of Québec and British Columbia, they had to threaten secession before they got what they believed was just. Far from Britain taking the side of "strong central government," it was a liberal era, and the Judicial Committee of the Privy Council, the final court in deciding Canada's constitutional questions, consistently supported provincial rights and offered a confederational interpretation of the BNA. Perhaps the most important ruling was that of Lord Haldane, delivered in 1919 as part of a judgement that confirmed the right of provincial governments to call initiatives and referenda, highly confederal procedures. Haldane said:

> The scheme of the Act passed in 1867 was thus, not to weld the Provinces into one, nor to subordinate Provincial Government to a central authority, but to establish a central government in which these provinces should be represented, entrusted with exclusive authority only in affairs in which they had a common interest. Subject to this each province was to retain its independence and autonomy and to be directly under the Crown at its head. Within these limits of area and subjects, its local legislature, as long as the imperial government did not repeal its own act conferring this status, was to be

supreme, and had such powers as the Imperial government possessed in the plenitude of its freedom before it handed them over to the Dominion and the Provinces, in accordance with the scheme of distribution which it enacted in 1867.

In other words, each province within the area of its own jurisdiction had inherited the sovereignty which the Imperial government was abdicating under the BNA, so the result was not an imposed federation but a willing confederation.

To continue and fulfill this process, I am now suggesting, is the task that Canadians face. It has become clear in recent years, and especially in recent months, that Canadians are angered by their alienation from the process of political decision making. Once again, but even more widely than in the 1960s, there is a call for a participatory democracy in which the individual citizen will have a far greater say in the administration of his country than in the past; that demand comes not from an alien minority, as it did three decades ago, but from people of all ages and conditions. More than ever, professional politicians are despised and distrusted by ordinary citizens, who think they could do better themselves. The time has come for the elevation of the confederal plan to a third, local level of decision and administration, subject directly to the sanction of the sovereign individual. (Considerable thought will have to be given to redefining sovereignty: how far should it belong to groups, how far to individuals?) Once we recognize this necessity and opt for an open confederation as a beginning, and as a model for ourselves and the world, then what appear to be our greatest problems—French-speaking Canadians both within and outside Québec, and Native peoples—may become transformed

16

into assets, contributing to the creation of a harmonious pluralist society, a model for the world. Given good fortune, our vast resources, our wonderful diversity of land and peoples, it is surely a duty and will equally surely be a privilege to find such a solution. People of the future will despise us if, given our advantages, we do not.

This will perhaps take more than the present weakening surge of constitutional argument and negotiation, doubtless soon to end in some makeshift political solution before this book is even published. But the evident failure of our present constitutional debate may be the ground on which will be built a new and exemplary social contract. Some polity has to fulfil the role Athens met in the Periclean age. It might be Canada, if only we were able to find our Pericles.

V

THIS IS NOT A WORK OF HISTORY or a political treatise. The times demand less deliberate approaches, and what I offer is the informal structure of a group of eight essays. They can be regarded as the late thoughts on Canada's possibilities, of a writer concerned with political thought in general for sixty years, and with the collective history of Canada for decades. If its readers choose to regard these essays as a kind of legacy, I shall not, at eighty, protest. At such an age, I find the mood is for giving.

The eight essays follow a figuratively confederationist pattern, for each is an autonomous discussion of special problems relating to the socio-political future of Canada, yet they follow a natural sequence with some cross-referencing and an evident movement of thought toward the final vision I have to offer.

In the first two essays, I shall be contesting two false principles that seem to lie at the heart of our present political practices, as distinct from what might be our true life as a society. One is the enshrinement in our parliamentary, judicial and even industrial relations of the adversarial system, sanctified by centuries of law and custom, yet a principal means of hardening differences between community groups, thus hindering the emergence of any fluid and consensual substitute. Lawyers joust like medieval knights, intent on personal triumph, rather than on the justice of their arguments or the fates of the people they prosecute or defend. Legislative bodies are divided into firmly defined and mutually antagonistic parties. And all this has encouraged rather than diminished tensions within society, for where victory is sought, rather than justice and mercy, whether in legislatures or in law courts, the willingness of people to respect each other without coercion is clearly diminished.

In the second essay, I pass on to the idea, overtly encouraged by politicians and by some political journalists, and somewhat slavishly echoed by some of the people, that what Canada needs is "more good leadership," or merely "more leadership." I argue that the preoccupation with leadership, and the existence of a party system dependent on such a concept, are the two principal barriers to accepting a more just and efficient system based upon the full participation of citizens in the administration of matters directly concerning them. I suggest that five-year parliaments and the current principles of leadership have propelled Canada in the direction of totalitarian rule.

The third essay deals with the situation among the native peoples, contrasting their characteristic political concept of

18

consensus with our adversarial attitudes, and their concept of the role of the chief with our concept of the role of the leader. I shall argue that Native traditions of self-government suggest it is high time we end state wardship of them under the Indian Act, and encourage the various tribes and peoples to establish their own autonomous administrations; we have much to learn from Native political capabilities, and any negotiations regarding the empowering of the Indian and Inuit peoples should become an occasion for educating other Canadians in the basic and natural democracies of unpolitical societies.

Since decentralization, apart from being so widely discussed in the world today, is an essential aspect of confederation, the fourth essay goes beyond self-government to consider the recognition of regional societies that are distinct culturally as well as geohistorically. The recognition of Québec alone as a distinct society would in fact be a distortion of the true situation, and in my view a harmful one. There is an outdated tendency to see Canada as formed of two blocks, the French-speakers, mostly in Québec, and the English-speakers in the rest of the country (apart from the territories and northern Québec, where the Native peoples generally predominate). But neither culturally nor historically is there such a thing as a homogenous English-speaking Canada. Several of the provinces have quite long pre-confederate histories, and—apart from language—there is as little in common between a Newfoundlander and a British Columbian as there is between a Québecois and a Prince Edward Islander. Essentially, English-speaking Canada consists of six regions with their distinctive histories, geographical conformations and cultures; these are Newfoundland, British Columbia, the Maritimes, the prairie provinces, Ontario and the northern territories.

This leads to the subject matter of the fifth essay. For however much we may divide Canada into major culturally distinct units, there remain the problems of distinct communities within regions. Some of these are highly evident, like the Acadians in New Brunswick, the French-speaking minorities in Manitoba, Alberta and Maillardville, British Columbia, and the Chinese and Sikh communities in Vancouver; others are minute but very distinct, having their own economies and rules of conduct, like Hutterite communities and Doukhobor settlements. But beyond these, there are the ordinary communities represented by some form of municipal administration from the village to the city. In Switzerland, such communes form the solid base of the political pyramid; the difficult process of becoming a Swiss citizen begins with acceptance by a commune. In Canada, municipalities have virtually no autonomy—even their by-laws are often subject to the approval of provincial legislators—and so our great cosmopolitan cities, like Montréal and Vancouver, are dependent on the whims of rustic politicians in petty capitals like Québec City and Victoria.

Decentralized societies—and countries as large as Canada—are more dependent on effective transport and communication links than smaller and more compact societies, because their populations and their essential functions are dispersed; that is a reason why decentralized Switzerland has the most efficient railway and village bus systems in the world. My sixth essay discusses the importance of transport and communications in sustaining a country as large and loose as Canada. The cultures of the various regions are linked to broadcasting systems, which should be flexible and locally sensitive. Some constitutional provision should guarantee that railway and air services, broadcasting and mail services are no longer reduced arbitrarily and without reference to local needs and historic rights.

A country's internal and external politics are intertwined in ways the seventh essay explores. Increasingly, for example, environmental problems percolate across frontiers. Events far away deeply affect our climate, as appears to be happening through the destruction of the Amazonian rain forests; the clearcutting of our woodlands may be doing the same for yet other countries. Old style professional foreign services are helpless in such situations, since they lack the proper expertise. Forest regions in Canada and elsewhere should be able to establish direct contact about shared environmental problems; the simple idea of twinning communities might be developed constructively in an increasingly decentralized world. We must recognize that the very pride of our sovereignty requires that our independence not be interpreted to the disadvantage of neighbours, human and otherwise, who share the planet with us. The Arctic must be protected, regardless of boundaries and sovereign claims, and we should be working with countries like Brazil and Indonesia in the shared task of preserving woodlands of world importance.

Inevitably, considering international relations, one comes to military alliances as distinct from peaceful co-operation. I suggest it is a matter of constitutional importance that a country should not become subordinate to a military alliance dominated by a greater power; the neglected matters of neutrality, and the importance of turning our armed forces into active peace forces, demands consideration in the present context.

Finally, there is the matter of ways and means. In the eighth essay, I present ideas on how a more complex yet more open three-level administrative structure with maximum popular participation might work. A number of thorny questions arise with this last idea, particularly in regard to civil disobedience—*technically* criminal acts—whereby so much progress toward human freedom has been made: should there be constitutional provision for the decriminalization of acts of justifiable civil disobedience? Should political crimes be treated separately as they were in nineteenth-century liberal Europe? For the civil disobeyers of yesterday often uncomfortably become the secular saints of today. The ghost of Gandhi haunts the law courts of modern democracies.

1

DING DONG!
OR,
KNIGHTS IN RUSTY ARMOUR

I

I HAVE TAKEN DOWN FROM MY SHELVES an already half-forgotten book which stands as a token of the instability of Canadian self-images. It is called *Canada: The Peaceable Kingdom*; edited by William Kilbourn, a popular liberal historian and municipal politician a generation ago. It was published in 1970. It presents an idyllic picture of Canada as a harmonious model for a world still given to conflict; in our uncertain and bickering 1990s, most of Kilbourn's successors will find his vision surprising, almost incomprehensible.

The "peaceable kingdom" he offers is not, indeed, the famous American primitive landscape, peopled by friendly Indians and Quakers and contented ruminants, from which he takes his title. But it does offer an extraordinary picture of a land full of promise and goodwill and confidence, and of examples for other less fortunate nations. It projects a vision that many Canadians once held in one way or another, especially during the Diefenbaker–Pearson era when, despite the gusty jousting of those tin-armoured champions, Canada seemed to offer the twin images of spreading social welfare internally and peacemaking externally. It then seemed possible that as Laurier (for Kilbourn, the most inspired of Canadian prime ministers) prophesied, the future might belong to Canada. Kilbourn distilled the feeling of the book, written by a great variety of Canadian and foreign observers (including a less experienced and cynical version of the present writer), when he remarked: "I cannot help feeling, along with many of the writers represented in this book, that Canada, merely by existing, does offer a way and a hope, an alternative to insanity, in so far as there is a hope for any of us in an insane world." It was, perhaps, a smug, complacent book, but it was also a smug, complacent period, for Canada at least.

Canada: A Guide to the Peaceable Kingdom was in fact one of the last manifestations of a period of intense euphoria, as Canada moved in 1967 into its second century, whose advent it celebrated in that extraordinary feast and fête of the imagination, Expo 67, and in an extraordinary creative outpouring in literature, theatre and the visual arts. Canadians—survivors by nature, as Margaret Atwood argued round about this time—responded to the feeling of having made it for a hundred years through all the problems of a vast land with a small and in some ways irrevocably divided population. The hope, the pride, the sense of a shared destiny continued for a few months after Expo, even a year or so, and then, in 1970—the very year that Kilbourn's book appeared—two acts by shabby terrorists, and the impetuous arrogance of a prime minister, combined to bring back the clouds of Canada's customary adversarialism—the condition on whose dissolution any successful attempt at a political harmonization depends.

A cell of the urban guerrilla movement of Québec nationalists known as the Front de libération du Québec (FLQ) captured the British trade commissioner in Montréal, while another cell seized one of the leading provincial Liberal cabinet ministers. The provincial minister was eventually found murdered, but before that happened Pierre Trudeau, as prime minister of Canada, had reacted with a melodramatic arrogance, declaring that an insurrection was imminent, invoking the iniquitously autocratic War Measures Act, ordering a military occupation of Montréal and Ottawa, and arbitrarily interning some hundreds of Québecois radical politicians and unionists, artists and intellectuals, against whom not a single specific charge could or would be laid.

These events in October 1970 revived all that was adversarial in the Canada of the self-styled "founding peoples." In Québec, they made the eventual (1976) victory of René Lévesque and his Parti Québecois inevitable. They created an unreasoning fear among English Canadians, so that even so sensible and decent a man as the poet and constitutional lawyer F.R. Scott personally offered his support to Trudeau's acts of rash tyranny. Those of us who had been influenced by the euphoria of 1967, and perhaps had contributed to Kilbourn's guide to the peaceable kingdom, withdrew into watchful neutrality. Everything in our libertarian consciences was repelled by the actions of Trudeau, that renegade confederationist who now dismissed all who protested against his actions as "bleeding hearts." The white man's Canada of the hopeful 1960s had sunk back into its customary antagonisms. And we began to fear that the adversarial attitudes which had continued in our political and judicial relations might be the habitual, if not the necessary, condition of our public lives.

II

INHERITED FROM EUROPEAN and even from some Asian traditions that Canadians sustain, the adversary position is stubborn and self-perpetuating. Its tendency to recur in times of crisis may be one of the principal reasons why, with so much in our favour, we have failed for 125 years to evolve for our society the formal model of a constitution suitable for our local genius and our pluralist inclinations. Adversary relations mar the Canadian polity in many directions—in the search for justice and mercy in the courts, in the relations between workers and employers, and in the search for a compassionate and economically effective society through political means. I suggest that the adversarial principle and its manifestations are the principal enemies of an effective harmonization of interests in a country like Canada. If I thought there were no way of modifying them, no countervailing process, I would not continue any further with this book. But my reading of Canadian history tells me that a kind of dialectic is at work in our society which up to now has in the long run balanced adversarialism with compromise, consensus and co-operation. We have never been a revolutionary country; however, as I showed in my earlier book, *The Century That Made Us* (1989), we have been a country in which adversarial stances have led to rebellion, although almost invariably there has been eventual reconciliation, the triumph of consensus, conciliation. This gives me the hope to continue speculating on the future of Canada and continuing to engage myself in its critical debates.

III

I SHALL RETURN LATER IN THIS CHAPTER to the general importance of conciliation in Canadian history; the next chapter deals with the adversarial defects of our system of "representative" democracy, and later I shall consider the antagonisms between First and Later Peoples. First, I will turn to the other areas where adversarialism has so broadly and negatively prevailed: the administration of the legal system and the fundamental relationship between workers and employers on which our economy depends.

The investigation of crime and the administration of what we hopefully call justice are always in practice—if not in nature—inclined to be adversarial, largely because that serves the interests of so many people. Apart from the lawyer's fees and the cop's perquisites, which flourish on conflict, there is an encouragement of adversarialism in the assumption from which every prosecutor argues that the state is always right; so crime and its prevention are really a duel between good and bad, between the agents of society, from policemen to judges and the individuals who are seen as its willing enemies.

It is true that in the British system of justice, from which the Canadian derives, there is a set of what one might call judicial Marquis of Queensberry rules to ensure fair play, such as habeas corpus and the presumption of innocence. But these are part of an old concept of popular law of which juries were once an integral part, sometimes virtually changing the law and implicitly condemning the Parliament that passed it, by refusing to convict whatever the evidence; this happened in England when capital crimes became too numerous. In Canada, however, the triumph of the Gallic idea of codified law has strengthened its coercive side and, hence, the adversarial element in its administration. George Orwell, who had served as an imperial police officer, once remarked that the policeman was the natural enemy of working men. Whether that is true or not, the police are indeed ex officio enemies of all individuals who defy the state or society's current mores, as given expression in its laws, even though defiance may be based on principle. Like their dogs, they are trained to catch real criminals and deter potential ones, thus creating automatically an adversary situation between them and social groups that, for various reasons, live outside the current accepted norm.

Faced with instances of brutality such as the one that produced the May 1992 Los Angeles riots, we often assume that policemen who perform violent acts are motivated by individual race or class prejudices. I suggest the cause lies more often in the adversarial situation itself; the policeman is dominated by an implanted impression, mostly the result of his training, that blacks are bred at a level of society where criminality, poverty and unemployment are endemic, and hence young men become desperate and dangerous. The natural corollary to this thesis is that young miscreants must be dealt with accordingly: to be shot if necessary, as one might shoot a mad dog. I believe also that the arbitrary mistreatment of Native peoples of which white Royal Canadian Mounted Police (RCMP) officers were so often accused in the past, may have actually happened, but had its origins less in racial contempt than in the policemen's perception of people whose way of life might be seen as improvident, disordered and even amoral by men or women who have dedicated themselves to a regulated existence.

The adversarial situation between police and potential criminals in Canada has been given a peculiar extremity by the quasi-military professionalism of Canadian law-keeping forces like the RCMP, which contracts the policing of most Canadian provinces and serves as a model for city forces and for provincial ones in Québec and Ontario. Apart from its origins as a frontier cavalry in all but name, the RCMP's mythical status as guard dog of the infant nation has marked and marred it for the past 125 years. Even in the lesser police forces, there is an esprit de corps that shelters the man or woman who goes too far in the zealous handling of suspects; there is also a career motivation that makes officers seek convictions not because they genuinely believe in the guilt of the accused, but so that they may gain credit and promotion in a service where courtroom successes are regarded as necessary for recognition. The unsolved crime becomes a challenge and a reproach, and even if they do not actually manufacture evidence, the police are often sorely tempted to distort what they have, or, as in the recently exposed Milgaard case, to apply varying degrees of pressure in their examinations and thinly disguised briefings of accused people and witnesses. Their relation with the world they perceive to be criminal is, in spite of the strange symbiosis between cop and crook that produces the stool pigeon, adversarial from the beginning and throughout.

The duel that goes on between prisoner and policeman in the station cells is repeated later in the courtroom, where defence and prosecution enter into a contest which consists of each lawyer breaking down without regard to its truth the evidence of the other side, and in winning points—not necessarily legal ones—that will sway the jury or the judge or both. In such contests, the judge acts as a kind of umpire between the champions, and the human predicament of the prisoner and/or his presumed victims is usually forgotten when the final decision is made by the jury and the sentence is handed down. Many a person has lost freedom, or even life, from the failure of his counsel to win a battle of wits rather than of facts.

IV

AS I WRITE, I CAN IMAGINE YOU, my literal minded reader, raising an admonitory hand and remarking that the misdeeds of policemen, and the weaknesses of judges or juries in the everyday conduct of criminal investigation and administering justice, are not matters of constitutional moment. But if we are to regard—as all democrats should—the main object of a constitution as being the best way of safeguarding the rights of the person, then I would argue that the judicial process is very much part of the constitution-maker's mandate. Even beyond the basic matter of safeguarding rights and freedoms in individual cases, I would suggest that that happenings in the streets and the cells and the courtrooms reveal negative attitudes to social relations, to compassion and fairness, that have an important bearing on the problems we may encounter in creating a less adversarial and more consensual way of administering our country.

In any case, the courts enter increasingly into the actual constitutional process, especially as Canada moves nearer to the American model in its development of the courts as interpretive institutions forming a counterbalance to the possible excesses of cabinet, parliament and bureaucracy. Thus, we all have an immediate interest in diminishing the adversarial factor that has always infected the practice of civil as well as criminal justice. Nobody, to my knowledge, has treated the removal of partiality from the judicial or police systems as a matter to be systematically considered in the constitutional debate; we are too bemused with political power and its distribution to consider the agencies that might help to curb and contain it. Yet the courts, like Parliament, are infected and somewhat corrupted by adversarial attitudes.

The judges in any Canadian court come up through the legal system with all its adversarial elements. This applies even to the judges of the Supreme Court who, to make matters worse, are chosen by the prime minister, the leader of the ruling party. They are not required to have any training in political science, though it is political acts on which they will often be passing judgement; and they are not expected to give proof of the kind of broad humanist background which encourages the qualities an ideal final judge needs, compassion and cultural tolerance.

Canada has, in fact, lost much by acquiring its own court of final constitutional and legal appeal. On constitutional matters it has always leaned toward the idea of strong central government, whereas the Judicial Committee of the Privy Council, judging in the objectivity of physical distance and unobliged for their appointments to the central government, were able to foster the confederalism implicit in the BNA.

In dealing with criminal matters, as in their recent hearing of David Milgaard's case, the Supreme Court judges too often close ranks, maintaining the esprit de corps of the penal-judicial system in Canada. Taking into account the police bullying of witnesses, the way in which the prosecution lawyers uncritically accepted the manipulated evidence, and the flawed direction of the trial judge, the Supreme Court ruling that Milgaard had been given a fair trial amounted to contempt of justice if not contempt of court on the part of the judges. The fact that they reached a decision that got Milgaard out of prison, while denying him the clearing of his name and the massive compensation which the state owes him, made their opinion particularly odious. Such situations will occur again and again unless our courts, from the top to the bottom, are changed.

What new system can we adopt? For obvious reasons, the system of prime ministerial or presidential appointment has failed, in the United States especially, but also in Canada. The election of judges, which happens in some of the American states, is one of the least effective of populist devices, leading to alarming possibilities of corruption. We have to make a new approach and to ask, first of all, whether legal training is needed. Legal training, after all, is—as we have seen—a training in adversarialism, and few lawyers rise above it. On the other hand, a man or woman of education and culture, placed unexpectedly in the position of having to administer justice with fairness and compassion, is often highly successful. A remarkable example was that of Roderick Haig-Brown, a writer and small farmer at Campbell River with a good English secondary education. A magistrate was needed at Campbell River, and nobody else in the community seemed to fit the position so well as Rod, except that he had no legal training whatever, and made up for it by reading the Criminal Code and interpreting it in his own way. He was a great success, famed on the West Coast for his Solomon's justice, his compassion for drunks and derelicts and Native people in trouble, his contemptuous strict-

34

ness toward those who killed endangered animals or committed environmental offences that came within the scope
of his police court. Yet he was so careful and exact that few
of his verdicts were challenged.

Surely in Roderick Haig-Brown's achievement we can see
a new model for a Supreme Court. It would be a court of
capable men and women unburdened by political or professional loyalties. It would be chosen initially by nomination,
but finally by lot, so that good people could be in the running
but the process would not be corrupted by electioneering.
Any person could be a candidate, but to ensure quality and
recognition, each nominee would have to be supported by
a petition of at least a thousand signatures. The nominations
would be sorted into French-speakers, members of the First
Peoples, and English-speakers. On the selection day three
barrels would confront three people picked at random from
the crowd that had gathered on Parliament Hill. The first
would pick one name from the First Peoples' barrel; the
second would pick three names from the French-speaking
barrel; the third would pick six from the English-speaking
barrel. Obviously, repute would play a part in the nomination stage of the process, and one would hope to see some
of our best minds on the final list. My own preference might
run something like this: Maria Campbell for the First Peoples, and for the English-speakers Margaret Atwood, Dennis
Lee, Alex Colville, Donald Sutherland, David Suzuki and
Richard Gwyn. I am letting my personal preferences lead
me on, that is evident. The ten members of the court would
be appointed for a maximum of ten years, with at least one
rotating out each year to preserve continuity and change at
the same time. The presidency would be rotating and annual, chosen again by dipping in the hat.

V

EXCEPT WHEN THEY RETURN ANNOYING VERDICTS, juries
are among the humbler species in the fauna of social institutions. Ancient in origins, dating back to the Indo-European tribes and to Athenian democracy according to Solon
and Pericles, they seem rather like marsupial zoological
relics, and it is often forgotten that they offer a social
mechanism that goes beyond the mere declaration of innocence or guilt in an individual case. A jury can—and sometimes does with entire legality in defiance of the judge's
instructions—deny a law that seems to have become irrational or inhumane with the evolution of public awareness.
This happened often in Britain in the early years of the
nineteenth century, when juries refused to convict under
the many hanging laws of the time. In Canada recently,
there was a fine series of instances in which juries in various
parts of the country refused to find Dr. Henry Morgenthaler
guilty when he was clearly and boldly defying the existing
reactionary laws regarding abortion.

But, apart from its occasional role as a factor in changing
law, the jury system has a special interest in the constitutional debate because it does offer us an ancient concept of
democratic practice other than the representative democracy our politicians pretend to follow. For, with its selection
of citizens by lot, and its placing a civic obligation on those
so selected, the jury offers an alternative to the elective
system which recognizes the competence of ordinary people.
Professional politicians play no role—unless the accident of
the lot selects them—and since the jurors are chosen privately by public officials, charisma, cunning and all the

other false criteria that play a part in elections do not count in their selection. Jurors are usually unwilling to serve, and on the whole this tends to reduce their liability to let partisanship enter their debates and decisions.

The problems of juries are directly and almost exclusively the inner ones of personality; how their members react to each other in an often highly emotionally charged situation when they are in jury room seclusion; how they react personally to the defendant. Also, it must be remembered that the jury, drawn theoretically as it is from ordinary working men and women, tends to reflect the mores of the time: brought together, its members will probably appear to be more moralistic, more strict and more reactionary than if they were encountered individually, particularly since they are afraid of appearing to be fooled by clever lawyers or cunning defendants. The atmosphere of a court of law, in other words, casts its deadening shadow over them and their special but temporary relationship.

But the jury—or the committee picked by lot—is an ancient institution, much used, for example, by the ancient Athenians in their experiments in direct democracy, and divorced from a criminal law situation it can serve in the settling of other matters, especially where a form of arbitration is involved, or those that arise when a town or a village or a small group of people meet to settle a matter of purely local interest.

I shall have more to say about juries, and the virtues in certain circumstances of choosing agents of the people by lot rather than by election, particularly when I discuss how to achieve and maintain the autonomy of regions, districts and communities in my fifth essay, "A Forest Survives Through Its Undergrowth." But before I pass on to that question, let me suggest that if we decided to be really democratic in our constitution-making and went so far as to create a constituent assembly, one way would be by lot, according to some plan modified to suit our regional and cultural distinctions, so that it would become a grand jury of the nation.

For what happens in the jury room is in fact a development of the consensus elsewhere lacking in our political and judicial systems, a reversal of the adversarialism that has flourished in the courtroom. The decisions of the juries may not always seem to us the right ones, and we may feel that the jurors have not entirely succeeded in escaping the current prejudices of their society, but at least the way they reach their decisions, arguing until the achievement of a precarious unanimity, shows the working of consensus, compromise and conciliation, all of them the opposites of adversarialism.

VI

THE ALTERNATION OF CONFLICT AND RECONCILIATION has been a special feature of Canadian history, and perhaps if we spend a little time examining it, we shall be getting close to the character of Canadian political life, and to the reasons why we should create, if we continue with the exercise, the most flexible of constitutions.

It has often been pointed out that, unlike the United States, Canada did not come into being as the result of a revolution. True enough; but we should not consider that proof that violence and anger have not played their parts in the development of our polity. At times, people in Canada have been so moved by anger and desperation that we can count no fewer than four armed rebellions within a fifty-year period of the mid-nineteenth century, Canada's formative age. Two took place in the eastern provinces in the 1830s as part of the struggle against the colonial oligarchies that then ruled both Lower and Upper Canada, and two in the West, during the decades when the remnants of Rupert's Land were being incorporated into the Dominion. The last of these uprisings, the North-West Rebellion of 1885, was the first time a truly Canadian army went into action, at Batoche in Saskatchewan, against other Canadians trying to preserve their lands and their other aboriginal rights.

In both areas, the final result was a reconciliation that moved Canada toward the kind of pluralist polity it must become. The results of the two rebellions in Lower and Upper Canada were not only the Durham commission and the subsequent attempt to absorb and anglicize the Québecois through the creation of a single province in Canada. More important was the frustration of the latter plan by the alliance that sprang up between Anglophone reformers led by Robert Baldwin, and Francophone reformers led by the former rebel Hippolyte Lafontaine, which led eventually to the end of imperial government over all the British American provinces, and to the creation of the Canadian confederation. A striking symbolic feature of this reconciliation is that the two rebel leaders, Louis-Joseph Papineau of Lower Canada and William Lyon Mackenzie of Upper Canada, returned unmolested from exile and were actually elected to the legislative assembly of the united province of Canada, in which their presence remained principally symbolic.

The first western rebellion of 1870, the Red River Rebellion, ended in the extension of the confederal principle to the West by the creation of the province of Manitoba, which for the next third of a century would be the sole outpost of political democracy in the prairie region, and eventually— although roughly a century later—to the acknowledgement that what the Métis and Indian rebels of 1885 fought for may at last be given concrete recognition. Rebellion, in other words, transformed into reform, has led to reconciliation, as aboriginal self-government is at last being seriously discussed.

Some of the most striking patterns of hostility and reconciliation in Canadian history have been racial and cultural ones. In later essays, I discuss the ways in which such considerations and their consequences affected the relationships between Native peoples and white peoples and between the Francophone cultures (Québecois and Acadian) and the majority Anglophone culture. Even more brutal in their initial phases, because their targets were regarded as intruders as well as being thought different and inferior, were the hostilities against successive waves of immigrants, some of whom, like the Irish, complicated the situation by importing the feuds of their homeland, so that for generations the cities of Canada were disturbed by skirmishes between Catholics and Protestant Orangemen.

Asian people were resented for many decades, particularly on the Pacific coast, and the general hostility towards the Chinese, who came with the gold rush of 1858 and again to take part in building the Canadian Pacific Railway, followed by the later-coming Japanese and East Indian Sikhs, was not merely ethnic but also economic. The labour unions blamed them for accepting low wages and poorer working conditions than white workers, and politicians, with an eye to the working man's vote, allied themselves to various anti-Asian movements, one of which provoked serious riots against the

Chinese and Japanese communities in Vancouver during 1907. The laws passed by the British Columbia provincial government to restrict the entry of Chinese were at first declared ultra vires by the federal government, but eventually Ottawa joined the movement of discrimination by passing laws that virtually excluded Chinese newcomers. After Pearl Harbor had aroused fears of an invasion of the Pacific coast of Canada, the Japanese were subjected to restrictions of movement, to confiscation of their land, boats and businesses, and to transportation away from the coast. As for the Sikhs, they had suffered dramatically in 1914, when the Japanese boat *Komagata Maru* endeavoured to land several hundred of them—all British subjects, of whom many had served in the army of the Raj—in Vancouver harbour. Eventually a ship of the newly founded Royal Canadian Navy, HMCS *Rainbow*, trained its guns on the *Komagata Maru* and escorted it from Canadian waters into the high seas. And so, if the Canadian army first went to battle against Canadians on the Saskatchewan River, the ships of the Royal Canadian Navy first went into action against British subjects who, in theory, had at least the right to land and settle in what, after all, was called British Columbia.

Yet despite this concentrated hostility on the part of people of European descent, and despite the often resentful stubbornness with which the Asians responded, conciliatory elements were at work. The Chinese continued to live usefully by providing services other Canadians did not offer, such as their market gardens, their neighbourhood green-groceries, their labour as gardeners and as domestic servants when European women were scarce for the task, their laundries, their shops and restaurants that formed colourful quarters in many Canadian cities and attracted tourists. The Sikhs entered the lumber industry, and some became wealthy mill owners while others operated an indispensable role as fuel merchants at a time when wood- and sawdust-fuelled furnaces were common. Even the Japanese, so savagely treated and thrust out of the fishing industry in which they had prospered, endured their persecution with a patience that touched many consciences, particularly when it became known that the federal and provincial politicians and bureaucrats (many of whom profited personally when Japanese properties were sold) had embarked on this cruel enterprise against the advice of the local security services, both RCMP and military intelligence. (Not one Japanese, whether born in Japan or in Canada, was convicted of spying or sabotage or even accused of either.)

Today, walking the streets of Vancouver or Victoria, of Toronto and Montréal, where Chinese and Japanese, East Indians and Caribbean blacks have become so visible an element in the population, it is hard to remember that these people, who play such an active role in Canada today, were still living in a political and social ghetto, even if not a physical one, until the years after World War Two. In 1947, the Asian groups were granted the federal franchise, and thus entered the Canadian community as first-class citizens. (This did not happen until 1950 for the Russian-speaking Doukhobors, whose sin had been to find original and active ways—such as parading nude—of reacting to persecution for their principles as a radical minority.)

The first step of reconciliation had been taken, so that at least in our Canadian constitution-making, we do not have to think in terms of first- and second-class citizens. The resolution of the problem of Asian immigration had to wait until Canadians had gone through another evolution in their collective thinking, another stage in their abandonment of adversarial relationships.

In our country's early days, before and shortly after Confederation, it was believed that the only acceptable peoples to add to the "founding" mix of British and French were those of northern Europe, of Teutonic and Celtic descent. Even some of the Celts, like the Irish who came in their plague-ridden hordes during the 1840s, the decade of the potato famines, were given scanty welcome, although they had played a great and necessary role doing the excavation work on the canals that provided the country's first even partially effective transport network. Icelanders, Pennsylvania Dutch, the true Dutch from New Amsterdam and the Hudson Valley, the Mennonites of German descent, fleeing from persecution in Russia, and the north Germans who founded the settlement of Lunenberg in Nova Scotia, all turned out to be industrious and enterprising additions to the country's population. But after 1870, when the vast spaces of Rupert's Land fell into Canadian hands and had to be settled to save them from American frontier greed, there were just not enough North Europeans eager to fill the great territorial void.

It was then that Clifford Sifton, as Laurier's minister of the interior, began to open the frontiers to what many people of English extraction regarded as the "lesser breeds," starting with the oppressed and discontented Slav peasants who were subjects of the Russian and Austro-Hungarian empires. These included Poles, Czechs and Slovaks, but the most numerous were the Ukrainians, called Galicians since most of them came from Galicia—then in Poland. Sifton's decision was widely criticized on mainly ethnic grounds, but he persisted, and in the years between 1892 and 1914 the prairie was populated. During the two wars and the Depression in between them, there was little immigration, but after World War Two the first comers were once again North Europeans—British, Dutch and Germans. When the job market of a rapidly expanding economy had absorbed these groups, it was the turn of the Mediterranean peoples: Italians first, and then Greeks and Portuguese. Finally, in the 1960s, immigration was opened to so-called visible minorities, the Asians and the peoples of the Caribbean. At each stage there was initial popular rejection of the newcomers, followed by reluctant acceptance, followed by a period of reconciliation as the immigrants settled down into the space that seemed to offer itself to them. (And there was always a space!)

It is this process of reconciliation and settling-in that represents the true core of what we call multiculturalism, a goal justified in the sense that it enables a culturally distinct group to continue sustaining its own collective identity at the same time as it contributes to the greater pattern—pluralist in every way—of Canadian life. (One of the observations that encourages me most on a trip to Toronto as a grudging Westerner, for example, is the good sense of the city fathers, who have recognized that their community is culturally diverse and in certain districts have instituted bilingual street signs; the two languages are not English/French, but English/Chinese, English/Italian, English/Greek. In this way, our essential diversity is used to unite and not to divide, and the adversarial image is replaced by the consensual one as the majority language loses its dominance.)

Apart from the traditional polities of the Native peoples, the increase in population by immigration is probably the area of Canadian existence in which reconciliation has most admirably emerged from an initial adversarial relationship.

Immigration is of vital importance in a country like Canada. It reinforces our garrison hold over a vast and still almost empty territory, and it has also, especially over the four and a half decades since World War One, greatly varied and enriched our culture. We have been able to offer the people who come by choice to live among us a chance to share the wavering fortunes of our economy, a guarantee of personal freedom and probably fairer treatment than they know at home, and the right, which we vaguely call "multiculturalism," to continue speaking their own languages when they wish and to follow their customs, so long as these do not drastically offend our natural proprieties; we draw the line, for example, at burning wives and eating clergymen.

That we should continue along these lines should be a basic Canadian assumption, for we have always gained by our hospitality to people of other origin who come like the gods a-visiting, and we have all in our turn—even the peoples we call "aboriginal" or "indigenous"—been immigrants in the prehistoric or historic past of our land.

Those who come out of free choice to our country must be welcomed wherever there is room to receive them, and those who flee from genuine tyranny must be accorded the brotherhood among people of all kinds that will make us the free and diverse society we aspire to create. Since, as our great and compassionate writer Margaret Laurence pointed out, we are all strangers in a strange land, by ancestry if not personally, we should insist that in any new constitution there be clauses that take strangers under their protection, so that no law may discriminate against them.

I would not like to see an eventual social contract without

a right to immigrate specified, and an equal right to remain something beyond a mere Canadian, for I am not one of those who would welcome a homogenous land, either in language or in custom. I believe the hyphen and all it implies are necessary in our diverse world, and I would say to immigrant groups: Contribute all you can! Keep all you need! If someone had thought of saying that at the turn of the century, for example, the Doukhobor problem would never have existed.

VII

CLASS WAR! THE LABOUR STRUGGLE! The phrases are practically as well as rhetorically familiar to Canadians, and they imply a special form of adversarialism that also may be moving toward conciliation.

Antagonism between employers and employed is almost a traditional Canadian relationship, depending on the relative militancy of the unions and the relative intransigence of the employers. Generally speaking, the antagonism was less bitter and less hard to resolve when craft unions of skilled workers were involved. The relationship between unionism and radical politics was not an inevitable one. In Canada, as well as in Britain, there were plenty of Tory working men, and the organized workers sometimes gained from the vagaries of political contest. In the early days of industrial organization in Canada, the old British laws against workers' "combinations," which had been repealed in England after Confederation, remained in force here. A major crisis was precipitated in 1872, when the quasi-legal unions showed their strength by great demonstrations organized by the Nine-Hour Movement (in many places of employment the actual hours of work were as high as twelve a day!) Several strikes accompanied the demonstrations; the most important was that of the Typographical Union against the Liberal leader George Brown's *Globe*. Brown was bitterly opposed to the unions, and invoked the obsolescent anti-combination legislation. The union leaders were prosecuted, but Sir John A. Macdonald, then prime minister, seized the opportunity to discredit his political rival, and introduced measures to repeal the anti-unionist laws. He gained both personal satisfaction and enough votes to turn several seats in the next election.

Antagonism between unions and employers was endemic throughout Canada until well after World War Two, and there was no really effective mechanism for conciliation. The adversarial relationship reached its height during the early years of the twentieth century, as the exploitation of natural resources in the Cordillera and on the Pacific coast led to an entirely different pattern of labour relations than existed between employers and skilled workers in the towns and growing cities of central and eastern Canada. Logging and hardrock mining were the main extractive industries that developed at the turn of the century, largely dominated by ruthless entrepreneurs, often American magnates who had gone through their own labour battles.

The western workers consisted largely of the homeless, unskilled migrants (in the double sense often of being both immigrants and modern-age nomads whom the old craft unions had mainly ignored). These "bunkhouse men" lived crowded together in logging and mining camps, and this daily proximity encouraged them to think collectively in a way men who left work each day for their individual family homes did not.

Out of this situation sprang the militant movement of industrial unions, of which the classic example was the IWW, the Industrial Workers of the World or Wobblies, who adopted many of the aims of European syndicalists of that period, including the revolutionary transformation of society by the workers' taking over the means of production and distribution. The IWW, or unions influenced by it, evolved highly activist methods and fought a number of militant free speech and industrial campaigns, in which the federal and provincial governments gave their moral and physical support to the employers. In Prince Rupert in 1912, even before the *Rainbow* had taken action against the *Komagata Maru* in Vancouver, sailors from the Royal Canadian Navy were used against striking construction workers, as much to intimidate the strikers as to protect property. The most dramatic of these government-employer-worker confrontations took place in the coal mining town of Nanaimo in late 1913, when striking miners took over the streets and paralyzed the working of the town. The provincial government mobilized a battalion of militia, and Nanaimo remained an occupied town until the outbreak of the Great War in 1914.

Wartime restrictions on union activity, increased opportunities for employment and other temporary circumstances slowed down militant activities for the duration of hostilities. But almost immediately the war was ended, syndicalist activity re-emerged, instigated this time not by the IWW, which had been eroded by persecution during the war years, but by other militant groups, which aimed at establishing a syndicalist-inclined One Big Union. The One Big Union never did materialize as an active body, but the agitation connected with it led to the most famous industrial conflict in Canadian history, the Winnipeg General Strike of 1919, which saw employers, the RCMP, the army, the federal, provincial and municipal governments all ranged against the strikers, who actually included some of the local police-men. The Winnipeg General Strike may have been the high point of industrial adversarialism in Canada, and it was perhaps inevitably defeated. A whole generation passed before the mutual hostilities it had bred died down, and the principle of collective bargaining, over which it had largely been fought, became established.

The present economic crisis has produced new reasons for conciliation. Where in the past both sides would grudgingly accept attempts at mediation, which often failed, forcing provincial and federal governments to legislate resentful strikers back to work, claims are now pushed more tenta-tively—except, significantly, in the public service where the taxpayer's pocket is naïvely regarded by both sides as bot-tomless—and strikes tend to become brief symbolic exer-cises, because even the most rabid class war fanatics realize how the rules have changed and how the general nature of the economy demands a caution unnecessary even a decade ago. Trade union bosses no longer go to prison in grand gestures of defiance, since they know it will neither assist their present struggle, nor will it provide that status as heroes—symbolic and often profitable as well, as it might once have done.

This softening of attitudes during the recent economic crisis has led some employers, many workers and a few union leaders to move in toward an area of consensus and concil-iation that had not seemed attractive to Canadians in the past; the three groups are beginning to see in many cases that their interests are ultimately not separate, and that the struggle to save a plant or a factory from closing down may be more important at this moment than either the profit interests of the employers or higher wages for the workers. If the workers need assurance of job security, that involves the viability and stability of the firms that employ them, and the best way to protect those is to prevent the closing of the plant or a mass layoff of workers. The employers need assurance of quality workmanship and increased productivity so as to compete effectively in the market, without having to pay for it in terms of uneconomically high wages and fringe benefits.

Plants in European countries, notably in Germany and Italy, where Olivetti was an early pioneer, have dissolved the traditional labour-employer adversarial relationship and have established a kind of industrial consensus by various arrangements by which the workers have a direct interest in the business success of their employer. Sometimes the workers participate as shareholders in the actual ownership of the factory, and sometimes they are just assured a share of the profits. In such plants, workers are encouraged to offer their suggestions for improving production methods, administration, marketing; there are already many companies on whose boards workers' representatives actually serve. Everywhere the effect of the change in relations between employers and workers has been positive. In the new atmosphere of conciliation and co-operation, disputes on the shop floor and in the industry as a whole can be settled amicably without the festering resentment left by an adversarial situation, no matter who wins. Workers do operate more willingly and quickly, less wastefully, and with attention to the quality of workmanship, once they know that part of the gain from their diligence within a well-run factory or service will increase their income and security. They are working for themselves and their children, and not merely for some faceless investor; the work becomes their work, the products in a deeper sense their products, and the pride of the old guild craftsmen in the excellence of their work is reborn. Most such "shared" factories, no matter what system they adopt, report greater industrial peace, greater co-operation among all the groups involved in production, less waste and pilfering, an increased quantitative production per worker, and a product of more reliable quality. They seem to look forward to the day of complete workers' control, and some are planning for it.

In recent years, this approach has been adopted increasingly in Canada, and for the first time it is happening without the protests of labour union leaders, who in the past opposed any mitigation of the adversary system in which they had habitually operated, and to which they owed their power and their often immoderate salaries. They had even divided themselves from social democrats and other socialists who thought that worker participation in running industries might be a real step forward. Dave Barrett, the New Democratic Party (NDP) premier of British Columbia in the early 1970s, is widely believed to have lost his bid for re-election in 1974 because the unions were alarmed by his support at the time for worker participation in control and profits.

The wind has changed to a different quarter, for not only are there spectacular instances, like the Algoma Steel Mills at Sault Ste. Marie, where consortia of workers have taken over quite large works, but also less ambitious situations where stalemates in collective negotiations have been broken by the workers' acceptance of a lower wage, or at least no increase, in consideration of a share in the profits. In such cases the workers have kept their jobs and have received more cash than they did before, as well as having the satisfaction of saving their places of work and seeing them made more efficient. Even union bosses are now accepting such arrangements and helping to implement them, with a growing awareness that the days of adversarial relations in the field of labour in Canada may well be nearing their end.

The reform of our law courts and our general police and penal system is clearly of great eventual constitutional importance, for these are matters on which we need guarantees as citizens. Labour relations lie more in that area of a social charter which some of the NDP leaders have suggested as an extension of the constitution. As they present them, unfortunately, the NDP proposals are framed in a national view dominated by old-style social democratic centralism, and would fit in neither with the open constitution I am proposing nor with the broad and positive social contract which I believe should accompany it, and which these pages will progressively reveal. Meanwhile, we have to deal with the corrupting reality of Canadian political practices, the practices of the parties and so-called leaders who are endeavouring even now to dominate the process of creating a new constitution to satisfy a disillusioned people.

2

FOOLS AND FÜHRERS: LEADERSHIP AND FIVE-YEAR FANCIES

I

IN THE CONDITION of continuing political irritability that began to emerge in Canada prior to the failure of the Meech Lake Conference, and was partly caused by the secretive way in which it had been conducted in a closed conclave of heads of governments, I have heard too often what strikes me as a contradictory refrain. "The country needs more leadership." In fact, as the Meech Lake incident itself showed, Canada has been subjected to too much leadership, in the form of elected politicians and appointed high bureaucrats taking upon themselves, in secret session, major decisions about the future of our country that should have been open to Canadians in general, and subjected to their approval.

Meech Lake has been followed, despite the anger it generated, by a series of other incidents clearly showing the arbitrary nature of our political processes. Without any national emergency being declared or demonstrated, the army was sent in to intimidate the Mohawk militants who were embroiled with the Québec provincial police. Canadian forces were sent into a war on the Persian Gulf without Parliament being called, in contrast with Mackenzie King's delaying a declaration of war against Germany and the dispatch of Canadian troops in 1939, until he had the approval of both legislative houses. And the packing of the Senate by Brian Mulroney, whatever its marginal legality, was an action of gross and insolent arbitrariness at a time when the Goods and Services Tax, whose passing it was meant to ensure, had long been demonstrably opposed by the great majority of Canadians. More recently, as if the politicians had not learnt from their setback at Meech Lake, there have been further conferences of federal and provincial leaders over the constitutional question to which neither Native spokesmen nor representatives of the tertiary, municipal levels of government have been invited. Canadians, I suggest, are still trying to evade their responsibilities by accepting the acts of leaders without developing their own political capacities, by continuing to empower their politicians while failing to empower themselves.

I come from a generation that learnt to distrust the whole concept of political leadership, and did so with good reason. Over the radio in the 1930s, we would hear the din of the Nazis chanting "Ein Reich, Ein Volk, Ein Führer" (One State, One People, One Leader) as they goose-stepped through the streets of German towns and cities with their arms raised in salute to that sinister comedian, Adolf Hitler. Elsewhere, dictators flourished under variant titles all really meaning "leader": El Caudillo, Il Duce. In Russia, Stalin was treated as a reborn tsar in the flattering verses of wretched poetasters like Demyan Byedny, and China would develop its own variant in its cult of Mao Tsedong as the Great Steersman.

We lived in a world of leaders, of merciless, ignorant men whose pomposity was equalled by their cruelty, and who used that Mephistophelian quality known as charisma, aided by a great deal of clever stagecraft and hollow pageantry, to guide their people into adventures that in the end were disastrous. In England then, we even had our own aspirant "leader" waiting in the wings, Sir Oswald Mosley with his Blackshirt thugs and their aggressive and provocative marches through the largely Jewish East End of London. And Mosley, we had to admit to ourselves with uneasy shame, was partly a product of the infighting for power in the Labour party. Something at least of the authoritarian side of socialist state worship had gone into the makeup of this potentially dangerous hollow man.

I wasn't living in Canada during the 1930s, but I cannot imagine that, apart from the tiny minority of Québecois who supported the fascist Adrien Arcand, there was much leader worship, particularly in the larger parties. Neither R.B. Bennett nor that sly schemer Mackenzie King was adapted to sway the masses by charisma and loud speaking, while to the most prominent figures of the early Co-operative Commonwealth Federation (CCF), notably J.S. Woodsworth, the whole idea of charismatic leadership must have been repugnant. Tommy Douglas's early appeal was not a charismatic one so much as that of an honest and compassionate man responding to the desperation of his people at a low point in their history and the history of the world, the Depression era.

Of course, ever since political parties began to coalesce in the mid-nineteenth century out of the loose and shifting political alliances of the early days of "responsible" government, the system has burdened us with leaders of a kind who head the government when their party is in office, and personify it when it is in opposition. But even flamboyant figures like Macdonald and Laurier, who made their own quasi-theatrical appeal to the populace, largely through direct oratorical contact, have little in common with the Canadian political leaders of recent years, the Trudeaus and the Mulroneys, whose styles of speaking, whose techniques of political manipulation, whose very appearance, are manufactured to suit the roles they play, so that they become replicas of the hollow men of American politics, and ultimately of the totalitarian political managers whose every gesture was devoted to the maintenance of power.

Every kind of leadership is perilous and carries the perils of autocracy, although the less the demands of leadership preoccupy the leader and dominate his party, the more humane and indeed the more positively beneficial the role becomes. Perhaps the best times in Canadian political life during the present century have been those of "soft" leadership, when party leaders like Diefenbaker and Pearson led minority governments and their power was effectively curbed and used for positive purposes under the pressure of smaller parties whose support they needed to remain in office. The social legislation of which, even in its diminished condition, we are still proud, and the mediative achievements in foreign policy many of us remember gratefully, took place at such periods of soft and limited leadership, when the power urges of the leaders and their associates were effectively kept on leash. What was happening, of course, was a kind of power truce in which the more positive urges in society, as distinct from the more narrowly political aims of the parties, had a chance to develop within the parliamentary setting. Strictly speaking, these were situations in which leadership was neutralized and a degree of consensus was allowed to develop, resulting in generally beneficial rather than partisanly advantageous decisions.

The cult of leadership encourages and promotes and is also fed by the leadership conventions which, with their circus-like ambiance and their air of squalid intrigue behind the public brouhaha, sometimes—as in the most recent NDP convention—result in embarrassing inner-party scandals. Such shenanigans lower the image of the political process even further in the public eye, so that fewer and fewer capable people with a true awareness of social morality present themselves as candidates. From the universal contempt that builds up around politicians, even the best inevitably suffer, and one shakes one's head at his folly when a friend who cannot be suspected of corruptibility chooses to enter the race. Such occasions as the leadership conventions, obscene and undignified at their best, are borrowed from the Americans, whose political ballyhoo once aroused only a sense of superiority among Canadians. And they are closely linked with developments in the Canadian party and parliamentary systems that lead nearer and nearer to an American presidential system, but without the check on presidential power that exists in the United States through the election of a new Congress every two years, and through the freedom of congressmen and senators to vote according to their own opinions even if it means voting against the supreme president-leader.

II

ONE OF THE REASONS I AM CONCERNED about the recent growth of the cult of leadership in Canadian politics is that parallel to it there has been a perceptible shift toward authoritarianism—even autocracy—in the Canadian parliamentary and party systems. At one time I used to remark—and roused considerable agreement—that the RCMP, with its paramilitary disciplines and loyalties, would be the perfect instrument for a dictator if one ever were to emerge in Canada. Now I would say that an overt dictatorship is no longer necessary in Canada for those who seek absolute power, for our traditional but outdated electoral procedures and new developments within and outside Parliament are opening the way to a quasi-totalitarianism which, for lack of a better name, I would call five-year fascism.

Let me start with the question of the parties. What has happened is a steady tightening of internal discipline and a growing rigidity of structure. In the early days of Canadian parliaments, the systems were so fluid that political leaders like Sir John A. Macdonald and his provincial counterparts were perpetually occupied with gathering their "loose fish," as they called them, the Members of Parliament of independent minds or independent interest, and therefore not of unquestioning loyalties. Eighty years ago, Sir Wilfrid Laurier, that most clever of cajolers, came a political cropper when Clifford Sifton and Henri Bourassa led away their respective groups of loose fish out of the Liberal shoal over the issues, respectively, of free trade (then called reciprocity) and Québec nationalism. (The issues of the early part of the twentieth century were remarkably like those which have surfaced to trouble us as the century draws near its end.) And Sir John A., of course, suffered large defections over the matter of the Pacific scandal in the 1870s, when many Tories broke rank and deserted him in a way that would be unthinkable under the present party structure.

They were not particularly edifying times, for every MP seems to have given his allegiance in anticipation of benefits to be received, and Bishop John Strachan of the notorious Family Compact was able to look in 1848 at the so-called democratic system that had succeeded it, and to say: "All is party and, I may say, all is corruption, and it matters not which faction is in power."

"Power" remains the operative word, and patronage remains a constant factor, as it always was in Canadian politics; unless they are caught in blatantly criminal activity, politicians do not retire into poverty, and Mulroney's recent appointments to the Senate were a calling to the trough as blatant as Trudeau's on the eve of his withdrawal from politics. Patronage now is no longer the bait for the uncommitted but the reward for good behaviour, for obedience, and the contemporary parties are quite different organizations from the rackety old fish traps that the Victorian and Edwardian politicians operated. They are rigid, pyramidical structures of power that have changed parliamentary procedure as well as life within the party. The organization, in Parliament and outside, is bound by loyalties as strong as those that keep together a Mafia family. As Mel Hurtig remarked recently in *The Betrayal of Canada*, "although the nation is disintegrating the party comes first."

III

AT THE TOP OF THE PYRAMID sits the leader who, when he reaches office as a presidentially inclined prime minister, governs where he can by extra-parliamentary procedures like orders-in-council. Beneath the prime minister, ambitiously aping his style and watching his weaknesses, comes the inner circle of higher ministers who collaborate with him in weaving the shifting web of policy. Below stand the cabinet in general, largely dependent on the high civil servants who help turn policy into practice and make sure there are no revolutionary changes in administrative traditions. And at the bottom is the caucus, so highly disciplined from above, as recent events have shown, that a single vote against the party line can lead to expulsion, which for a politician means the loss of present perks and future prospects for advancement. It is a system as impervious as it is rigid. Despite freedom-of-information legislation, secrecy veils all its operations.

Below the whole structure lie the people, allowed to vote every five years and unheard in the intervals. Folk wisdom has well observed this fact. On tramps through the English countryside, one would occasionally come across an inn at a crossroads called The Four Alls. The sign, first painted perhaps a century and a half ago, at the time of the Reform agitations, would portray a man, meanly dressed, straining his muscles to hold up a round platform above his head. In the towns he would look like a millworker, in the country like a farmer on the edge of bankruptcy. On the platform, in gilded chairs, would be sitting a king (or someone of equal rank), a bishop and a general, all in their respective regalia.

From each of their mouths a ribbon of speech would come: "I govern all!", "I pray for all!", "I fight for all!" And out of the strained lips of the ragged Atlas below would come the words, "I pay for all!" The signs were always kept well painted; people believed in their message.

We also pay for all. The original painter of that sign and the radical innkeeper who commissioned him live at the end of an age when power was openly held by a few people. But a minority still rules us—part elected and part appointed— and we still dance with its burden on our heads and with the knowledge that all—even if they pay for all—do not even now have a fair share in ruling all. Today, it is rarely that a government has the support of a true popular majority. Seldom is a government elected by even 50 percent of the vote. Brian Mulroney in 1988 gained 169 seats in a 296-seat parliament with 43 percent of the popular vote; the remaining 57 percent of the actual voters (leaving aside the millions who had decided there was nothing to gain by participating) were represented by 127 seats, a shade over 40 percent. He has been in office for over three years since the 1988 election (and a total of eight years), and his government, as the polls repeatedly and consistently tell us, has, early in 1992 as I write, less than 20 percent support among the people.

IV

HOW THEN, AS IS CUSTOMARILY EXPECTED in a democracy, do the Canadian people govern themselves? Canadian historians have talked a great deal about "responsible government," and the struggle for it by the early reformers like Joseph Howe and the Baldwins and Lafontaine has become something of a national political epic, surrounded by a great

deal of popular misunderstanding, for many Canadians believe that a responsible government is responsible to the
people. It is in fact responsible only to Parliament, and when
both Parliament and the ruling party are locked in the kind
of inflexible pattern I have been describing, the idea of
responsibility loses the sense of accountability that it originally projected; the governmental system becomes account-
able only to itself. The duality which even the American
system at least safeguards no longer exists among us, and the
party leader who has become prime minister appears increasingly in image and in fact as the autocrat who is able to alter
the party's policies at will and, during his time in office, to
introduce measures—like the Free Trade Pact and the Goods
and Services Tax—not proposed at the time of his election.
Party leaders like Trudeau and Mulroney are often accused
by their rivals of seeking to transform prime ministerial into
presidential powers. With due deference, I would argue that
contemporary Canadian prime ministers act as if they had
more than presidential power, since the legislators do not
have the kind of countervailing power that is provided by
the American system of checks and balances. And a strong-
willed prime minister can rule virtually as he wishes. (I use
the pronoun *he* partly because, up to now, we have had in
Canada no woman prime minister and only one woman
provincial premier, the Rita Johnston who briefly held office
in 1991 in British Columbia, and also because, even though
we do now have one female federal party leader in the NDP's
Audrey McLaughlin, the present federal party structure is
essentially paternalistic in character. Indeed, when one
considers how female rulers in the past, from Cleopatra
through Elizabeth I and Victoria to the late Indira Gandhi,
have governed through tough male ministers, it seems that

political structures, no matter who stands at their head, are essentially paternalistic in nature.)

So the role of the leader in Canadian politics is largely but not entirely to project a charismatic image which is exploited especially at election time, when its full use through the media might influence our patterns of voting. How importantly that highly cosmeticized personal image of the leader may be regarded is shown by the fact that the rise and fall in popularity of, say, Pierre Trudeau or Brian Mulroney have always been of greater concern to those who conduct public opinion polls than the people's view on all but the most sensational aspect of public policy. This is in striking contrast to a country like Switzerland, with its tendencies toward participatory democracy, where political personality is downplayed, and the president is chosen for just one year out of a federal council of seven. Once I was on a train that went through the St. Gotthard Pass from Luzern down to the Ticino and Italy. At a little station on the south side of the pass there was a band and a small crowd waiting, with those heraldic banners to which the Swiss are so addicted. A nondescript man got off the train and was greeted by the local dignitaries in their *tracht*. "Who is he?" we asked our fellow travellers. Nobody was quite sure, but then the conductor appeared and remarked that it was the president of Switzerland returning to his home village. He was, the conductor added, a Ticinese, for this was the year for the Italian-speakers to have the presidency. For two years out of the seven, one of the passengers informed me, it would go to German-speakers, and for two to French-speakers, and there was a seventh year when it might go to one of the tiny minority groups—the Romansch-speakers and the Ladino-speakers—if they had a distinguished man or woman around that year, but otherwise would go to the Germans. Like every Swiss situation where language was concerned, it had been worked out pragmatically without any obligation on people to speak or to have to read anything other than their own language. My little cup of shame for Canada ran over that afternoon when I asked my fellow passengers for the name of their president, and nobody—not even the conductor—knew, and I remembered the posturing figures in Ottawa and even in our provincial capitals, and thought of this man wandering over the country, recognized only in his native village, and reputed to cycle quietly to work in his quiet little medieval capital of Berne.

Charisma and the influence it acquires for a man or a woman tend to go hand in hand with the grasping for power. Every charismatic leader in history has tried to concentrate power around him, and this is perhaps why the uncharismatic style of Swiss leadership is associated with a kind of diffused yet direct democracy in which the people participate deeply. Leadership in Canada has, for the most part, been associated with an intrusive type of centralist authority that aims at virtually complete control over lawmaking and builds up a range of administrative devices by which the law can either be manufactured or circumvented. Virtually absolute power can be established through a representative system originally designed for the better expression of the voice of the people, that is Parliament. Only in times of minority government—when, as we have seen, the government is obliged to consult and bargain with the other minorities (usually in Canada with beneficial effects)—has there been a curbing of the actions of government, which in times of absolute majorities sees no threat but a relatively distant election. In this way is created what I call five-year fascism, with its pattern of decisions by one man or a small group of men and women that affect the present and future lives of millions of people in one of the potentially most fortunate countries on earth. "The foremost betrayal in Canada," Mel Hurtig says in the book that he actually calls *The Betrayal of Canada*, "is that our current leadership has been destroying our freedom." True, it has, but no less blatantly than Pierre Elliott Trudeau's government, no less slyly than Mackenzie King's government. The fact is that all governments have in general militated against the freedom of Canadian groups and individuals since the Fathers of Confederation (one wonders what mothers might have done!) so uncritically accepted the mechanisms rather than the philosophy of representative democracy.

V

THE FIVE-YEAR TERM for the English Parliament originated in preindustrial England at a time when time moved slowly in a society only just familiar with the clock and still untouched even by the steam engine. Parliaments did not stay long in session, and the legislation they handled was minimal; their main function was to make sure that taxes were gathered with at least the indirect approval of the people, and it was over taxation that Parliament actually took up arms against King Charles I, whose neck, in the end, was not stiff enough to withstand the axe.

By the early nineteenth century, discontent was growing rapidly with the original parliamentary system, which tied suffrage to the ownership of property. Fanned by the gale of the French Revolution (which turned out in the end no real model of democracy), the idea that each man (though not yet each woman) must have his say spread rapidly, and with it went a strong desire to make sure that no political group, party or otherwise, should become too deeply entrenched in power. This was the reason for the demand for yearly Parliaments that played such a prominent role in the propaganda of the Levellers during the Commonwealth and of the great radical movement known as Chartism during the 1830s and the 1840s.

The Chartists saw the problem in terms of entrenchment of power: change the people's representatives often and you would not leave them time enough to become corrupt or arrogant. But now we can see the five-year parliament not only in terms of the entrenchment of power (which, as I have shown, has taken place through the rigidifying of the party system), but also in terms of the acceleration of events and developments in the modern world. Technologically, and in terms of social and cultural evolution, five years can witness immense changes, changes—as recent events in Europe have shown—that can be virtually unpredictable and yet alter the whole face of world politics. If the politicians kept to their original five-year programs, many of their measures would be out of place or out of date by the end of the period, and so they are tempted to introduce measures not in their original platforms; these must be "sold" to the people (who have no real choice about what is happening) in the hope that with a mixture of blarney and charisma, the leader may be able to gain their support. If he cannot, he will act in any case, as Pierre Trudeau did often and as Brian Mulroney does increasingly, operating as a kind of oligarchical tyrant, relying on his disciplined cabinet and caucus to push his plans through Parliament, and on the bureaucrats to impose them.

After the Chartists with their idea of annual parliaments, many radicals and populists have sought remedies for this situation of concentrated power, whose evils are aggravated by the fact that even when they are elected, our MPs do not represent all or even a majority of the people. Rarely, as we have seen, does any government in Canada—federal or provincial—command as much as 50 percent of the popular vote. It will be seen how easily, as discontent sets in, the minority actually supporting the government can dwindle toward nonexistence as has happened to the Tory government in Canada in 1992. The demand for proportional representation is an old one, and now liberal nationalists like Mel Hurtig are advocating it, as radical populists did in the past. There are countries that have found a political *modus vivendi* which allows them to carry on very well with kaleidoscopic parliaments that have not seen a party with a majority for decades, even generations, and there is the benign productiveness of our own period of minority government. Proportional representation is just, and with goodwill it can be made to work. But talk about it has been remarkably muted during recent discussions on the Canadian constitution, and this is because all the three major parties have based their election calculations on the gamble of winning as many seats with as few votes as possible. It remains for the people, if they seek to be truly represented not only in Parliament but also in the acts of government, to demand this basic reform.

Other devices can be aimed at mitigating the bad effects of long parliaments and governments with highly concentrated power. There are the twin procedures of referendum and initiative, the first initiated by governments and the second initiated on the demand of substantial groups of citizens. I shall have more to say on this matter when I come to the more basic levels of government, those below—or perhaps rather outside—the more visible manifestations of federal and provincial government.

The people could also participate in government through the devices of "recall" and impeachment. The recall is a method by which the voters who first elected the official vote again to decide whether he should be removed from power—usually because of poor or non-performance. If the vote is carried, a new candidate is put forward. The recall, one of the principal demands of the populists in the 1920s and now of the Reform Party, is part of the constitution of a number of American states, and the late Social Credit government of British Columbia passed it into law. A parallel vehicle of public participation is impeachment, a process in which a public official is accused of misconduct in office, before a competent tribunal. The recent frequency of accusations of corruption—some of them proved in the courts—against federal and provincial politicians, in two cases going as high as a premier, suggest that it is high time recall and impeachment were lodged firmly into any document restructuring our political life. We must get rid of the dross!

With shorter parliaments, proportional representation, referenda on important issues, provisions for recall and impeachment, there is at least a possibility that the greed and power hunger of politicians might be curbed, and governments might at last be responsive, if not responsible, to the people and their wishes.

Nor should we allow our sense of being separate from the United States develop into a sense of superiority toward its political system; we can resist domination and yet learn, as the Americans learnt from various models in framing their constitution. There are two features of the American system that largely make up for the irresponsible and autocratic presidency. One is the pattern of two-year Congresses, with staggered elections for the senators, so that some continuity persists while the legislature as a whole is regularly swept of its dead wood, and cliques and caucuses are kept unstable. (Political scientists have not yet studied sufficiently the benefits of instability, as earlier remarks of mine have suggested.) Even more effective is the detachment of executive from legislative power under the American constitution, which allows even the caucus of the president's party, either as a whole or individually, to dissociate itself from his policies, and even to challenge his right to office, as legislators challenged Richard Nixon over the Watergate affair and finally drove him out. Whatever the efforts of the opposition, whatever the qualms of his supporters, a Canadian prime minister with an absolute majority has not been effectively challenged since the party rebellion that dislodged Sir John A. in 1873, although at least two in recent years have deserved to be so challenged for their loss of the people's confidence: Pierre Trudeau and Brian Mulroney. Unless he commits some flagrantly criminal act, the Canadian prime minister remains immune and as absolute in his actions as in his majority, the personification of leadership.

This is why I react so negatively when a spokesperson of what poses as the political Left in Canada, like Audrey McLaughlin federally, and the man I remember genially as Mayor Harcourt of Vancouver, now premier of British Columbia, appeals to me on a fund-raising drive as "your leader," as if I had asked for a leader to make up my mind for me. It is why I become so angry with those who, parrot-like, say that this country needs "more leadership" and lead me to remember the tramping feet and the menacing voices so long ago in an unhappy Europe, which even now has not awakened from all its nightmares, if one can judge from the recent emergence of neo-Nazi groups and the rise of racial hatreds in Europe.

What this country needs politically is less leadership and less partisan adversarialism; it needs more partnership, more consensus, more patience in resolving our differences, more participation by the people in the decisions that affect their lives, and a major reform in our institutions, like Parliament and the political parties, that will provide for such participation.

The prime lesson of Meech Lake and the arbitrary governmental moves toward constitution-making that have followed it is, I suggest, that we should seek means of putting aside the leaders and find ways of effectively conducting our own affairs as directly as possible. We have examples close enough from which we can learn, as the effective action of a Native chief, Elijah Harper, demonstrated in the downfall of the government's plans for an easy solution at Meech Lake. The Native peoples, when they intervened in this dramatic way, did so on the basis of different concepts of nationality and democracy from our own, concepts based on conciliation and consensus rather than on adversarialism and competition. We have to examine their ideas, for there is at this stage no prospect that a satisfactory Canadian political arrangement can be made without finally recognizing and meeting the demands of the Native people. But in considering their claims, we may find also some of the means to rid our larger society of its faults and contradictions.

3

FIRSTCOMERS AND LATECOMERS

Had Champlain, like his predecessor Cartier,
encountered first the Iroquois on the St. Lawrence
River and discovered their military strength and genius
for political organization, France might today be the
dominant power in North America.
  —Diamond Jenness, *The Indians of Canada*, 1932.

I

JENNESS'S STATEMENT HAS A SPECIAL IMPORTANCE for
me in the context of the book I am writing because, even
while his whole sad narrative, *The Indians of Canada*, is a
prophetic threnody on what he sees as the forthcoming
extinction of firstcoming peoples and their societies, he does
recognize the impressive alternative models of government
and of social organization that had been developed before
the coming of the Europeans, when he talks of the "genius
for political organization" among the Iroquois.

But he also sees it as incidental to white men's history, to
the struggle of the French, the English, the Dutch, for
domination in North America. If the French, he argues, had
recognized the political abilities of the Iroquois instead of
allying themselves from the beginning to the politically
lightly organized Montagnais, they might have turned them
into allies and emerged triumphant over the British. Jenness, we must remember, was writing in 1932—imperial

times when nobody could have foreseen that loss of the will to rule which since then allowed all the world empires to vanish except for the Chinese.

Whatever Anglophone or Francophone politicians may think and argue, the basic historic and demographic division within Canadian society has never completely broken down. It has been and remains one between Natives, whose ancestors occupied the country when Cartier and the anonymous French fishermen who preceded him arrived on the St. Lawrence in the early sixteenth century, and Europeans, who came afterwards with their own social mores and political structures, and those from the rest of the world. Because the terms must be clear when the relationship between these groups is examined politically, I have begun with a title which I hope comes nearest to distinguishing the two categories of true and birthright Canadians.

The firstcomers (or First Peoples, as they often call themselves) are those who arrived before the latecomers imported history in the sixteenth century. Until very recent years, they were called Indians and Eskimos. The word *Eskimo* was a derogatory term, used originally by their enemies, the Chippewa Indians, to describe those who rightly now call themselves *Inuit*—the people. The word *Indian* is not in itself disparaging, for the true Indians are a people of great and ancient civilization; the objection to it is that it is patently inexact, the result of an Italian seaman's optimistic error in identifying his landfall. The name has lasted so long in use in the Americas because to this day the people or peoples to whom it is addressed have developed no general name to describe themselves as a populace outside tribal divisions.

Most of the alternative terms used recently seem equally inaccurate or inadequate to define either the identity or the historic position of the people or peoples they describe. "Native peoples" falls under the criticism that it refers by definition to place of birth and one's rights in that land. Born in Winnipeg, I am as much a "native" Canadian as any Cree or Ojibwa born in Manitoba and have my own birthright there as they do. "Aboriginal peoples," meaning literally those who were here from the beginning, is equally unsatisfactory because it conveys the connotation of autochthony, that the people to whom it is applied evolved or were somehow created in the country they now occupy. But we know that the predecessors of all the pre-Columbian tribes and peoples of the Americas came originally through Alaska as immigrants: raiding hunters at first, in the wake of great post-Ice Age mammals, and then spreading over the rest of the continent. Correctly speaking, they were the firstcomers, who arrived about fifteen to twenty millennia—a mere notch in geological time—before the first of the Europeans.

It is possible, given the great prehistoric movements of peoples, that most of us—Indo-European latecomers and Mongol firstcomers—originated in the vast and once fertile spaces of central Asia, whose desiccation sent our forebears wandering into Europe and northeastern Asia. But through all these millennia, until the ominous reunion that took place when the Europeans reached the Americas, political and social traditions had been developing in disconnected ways on the two land masses of Eurasia and the Americas.

II

THE DIFFERENCES THAT EMERGED become immediately evident when we compare the different use of the word "nation" in the two contexts. The European concept of the nation-state, which developed in the sixteenth and seventeenth centuries after the decline of the feudal order, tended to be aggressive and expansive. George Orwell once made a useful distinction between nationalism and patriotism.

Nationalism, Orwell said, is inseparable from the desire for power. The abiding purpose of every nationalist is to secure more power and more prestige, not for himself, but for the nation or other unit in which he has chosen to sink his individuality. Nation-states, one may add, tend to be aggressive not only toward other nations in economic or military ways (in both in the case of the United States); they are also oppressive to those who do not fit the national mould, as any good Breton or Welshman will tell you about the French and English nations.

"Patriotism," for Orwell, meant "devotion to a particular place and a particular way of life, which one believes to be the best in the world but does not wish to force on other people. Patriotism is in its very nature defensive, both militarily and culturally." It is, I suggest, a variant of this patriotic concept that distinguishes the idea of a nation as projected by Canadians who call themselves the first nations. It is not the aggressive, all-embracing nation that they proclaim, and for which they seek the land and other rights that might give their polity a reality. Whatever else may have happened in that dark period of transition when the Native peoples were encouraged to aggressiveness by the policies of competing European powers and the greed of fur traders selling arms, First Peoples nationalism is no longer aggressive, and the chance of Indian groups tyrannizing over others, as has happened recently in a number of African countries with autocratic native traditions, does not exist in Canada.

Yet First Peoples patriotism—if we choose to change the terms—is defensive in the Orwellian way, as many recent incidents have shown when bands and tribes—mostly non-violently—have tried to protect what they considered to be their land and its natural heritage from commercial aggression by latecomers. Even the incident at Oka, with its melodramatic posturing and its almost wholly oratorical violence (and its one unexplained death), was essentially a civil disobedience operation that picked the wrong rhetoric. The bands and tribes that call for political equality and autonomy within Canada each seek a status based on traditions they already have; they want an enclave of self-government in which language and custom and the sense of being an entity peculiar to itself in the modern world can be cultivated. So keen is the sense of unique and disparate destinies underlying such an attitude, that only recently have the various first nations of Canada recognized the common strains that run through their individual demands for land and autonomy, and created effective countrywide federations of tribes and peoples.

Now, with this coming together of the First Peoples, it is time to take seriously Jenness's hindsight advice to Champlain and the French. Too long we have failed to recognize what treasures of political wisdom may lie in the traditions of our firstcomers, and what appropriate lessons such old wisdom may give to a country engaged in a vital struggle to reconcile its largely contradictory social and political forces without neutralizing them, which would mean a kind of communal death.

Unfortunately, though predictably, those who hold power in Canada at present are intensely jealous of it, and none of them more so than the federal and provincial political leaders, whether Francophone or Anglophone. Their idea of negotiating a better confederation—especially in the case of the first peoples—will be to give as little as the other side will accept, so that whatever talks may take place will inevitably be conducted on an adversary basis. Even the few established parliamentary practitioners—including NDPers—who look with some sympathy on firstcomers' aims will find difficulty in granting a degree of sovereignty to any group that might disturb the smooth working of the universally intrusive Welfare State.

They will certainly question how a swarm of small autonomous communities, even if their land claims are justified, can be fitted into the established structure of present-day Canada, even if the latter moves in the direction of a looser confederation. They will be reluctant to admit that the kind of consensual democracy at which the first peoples have always aimed may perhaps be superior to the representative democracy that—as we have shown in the last chapter—is in the present age revealing so many flaws. And they will resent the possibility that people who for so long have been excluded from the business of power-making and power-holding may be able to give them lessons in running a society co-operatively and without the use of power. They will reject the thought of people treated so long as wards of the state being introduced into the national debate, not merely as equal participants but also perhaps as mentors.

Yet any constitutional negotiations based on the idea of merely giving the first peoples the minimum they can be talked into accepting, in the spirit of hard-nosed capitalist bargain-making, will be pointless and quickly self-defeating. That was tried in the infamous treaties of the 1870s that alienated from the prairie and parklands peoples most of their hunting lands for derisory compensation, and the results, notably in the 1885 rebellion and its aftermath, were disastrous. One reason among many was that the "wardship" established by those treaties allowed the successive offices and departments dealing with "Indian affairs," on behalf of Sir John A. Macdonald's centralizing government, to interfere with and frustrate the traditional political processes of the first peoples (for example, by trying to substitute representative democracy for consensual democracy); they were also permitted to destroy the very ceremonial patterns that revealed the distinctiveness of first peoples' cultures: the potlatch of the Haida, the winter festivals of the Kwakiutl secret societies, the sun dance of the Blackfoot, the spirit dances of the Salish. It is obvious, to avoid even more disastrous failure, that from now onward negotiations between the first peoples and the rest of Canadians must be open, lengthy and conducted without any kind of *arrière pensée* on the part of the Anglophone and Francophone participants, which would virtually exclude professional politicians from the process. None of the repugnant pressure tactics so ineffectively used by Prime Minister Mulroney at Meech Lake must be attempted; the role played by Elijah Harper and his fellow chiefs among the Cree in frustrating that agreement must not be forgotten, for they acted with skill, foresight and integrity. They gave us a chance we must not miss of new and fair negotiations, as well as a lesson in good Gandhian tactics of non-co-operation.

The new negotiations, when they take place, must be based not merely on the idea of how to fit the first peoples, with their special requirements, into a new confederation whose general shape has been determined by the two major latecoming peoples. Now we must all—firstcomers and latecomers together—be prepared to listen to each other as we play the greatest of all political chess games, the game in which everyone wins. Every effort at constitution-making in the past in Canada has left vast residues of resentment in large sections of the population—Québecois, British Columbians, Maritimers, prairie people, first peoples, Métis, women, various minorities—and that is why we must take our time, no matter how urgent the situation may appear, to establish a complex pattern of understandings, so that when we have finished we can offer to the world the model of a fair and decent society, pluralistic and libertarian.

The process should be one of learning, with on all sides a willingness to understand, to accept, to adopt and adapt. For example, instead of reacting with hostility to the demands of the Québecois for status as a distinct society, we should consider these demands in the light of the palpable distinctness not only of all the first peoples, but also of all our regional societies within English-speaking Canada; it is not two linguistic monoliths that must enter the new order, but a mutually harmonious consort of cultures well defined by history and geography.

And, having generally reached a conclusion that the system of representative democracy on which we once prided ourselves has failed to meet demands of the late twentieth century, it is surely time for us to consider all the alternatives, and to see what we can learn from the political forms that in their own special wisdom the First Peoples of Canada had evolved by the time Cartier arrived, and Champlain—according to Jenness—made the wrong military and political choices.

III

HERE, I SUGGEST, we have to move tentatively and in an exploratory spirit, for we shall begin as human beings learning about each other with few and mistrusted preconceptions. We have to know ourselves and the others before we can live fully together, and the Canadian past has not encouraged conversation or comprehension between firstcomers and latecomers. Hence, any negotiation that takes place must be intertwined with mutual enquiry and growing understanding.

The political system in Canada until now has been arranged so that the people who should be the true "insiders" in our world because of their immeasurably longer experience of the land, have been thrust to the periphery, only treated as Canadian citizens for the past thirty years or so, and even now regarded as irrelevant to the imported European culture that pushes them aside. Their geographical isolation, mostly relegated to remote and infertile reserves, has manifested literally and symbolically the role as outsiders that most of us accord them. The history of relations between firstcomers and latecomers has led to an exchange of resentments which it is hard to dissolve. The original goodwill with which Cartier was welcomed by the Iroquois of Stadacona was destroyed by 1536, when he kidnapped Chief Donnaconna and nine of his fellow tribesmen and took them to France, a journey none of them survived. The dawn of trust had been quick to fade, and the situation was not improved by the efforts of later French rulers to follow an assimilationist policy, sketched out when Minister Colbert wrote to Intendant Jean Talon in 1671: "Always endeavour by every possible means to encourage the clergy to bring up in their communities as many Indian children as possible, so that being educated in the manners of our religion, and in our customs, they, along with the settlers, may evolve into a single nation and so strengthen the colony."

Conversion did work to an extent on a religious level, and today there is probably as high a proportion of pious Christians among Native peoples as among other Canadians, although their beliefs have often passed through Manichean filters. And even the converted remember a conquest less spectacular than that which the Québecois endured, but certainly no less demeaning. Some were never in fact defeated by the white man, for we had no really great Indian Wars like those of the Americans, but they were overwhelmed by white men's diseases or by such human-induced disasters as the extermination of the great buffalo herds, as happened to the proud tribes of the Blackfoot and Cree–Assiniboine Confederations. Others were defeated by being made dependent, like those northern hunting tribes in whose relations with the fur traders a kind of class system emerged rather like pre-Industrial Revolution capitalism in which, before the rise of the factory system, entrepreneurs would employ hand weavers to work in their homes and bring the produce of their toil to a central depot. In the same way the Indians spent much of the time they had formerly devoted to food hunting in trapping and shooting the animals for pelts which could be exchanged for products, like iron pots and tools, tobacco and alcohol, that made them more and more dependent on the traders for their needs. Whichever way their degradation happened, the Indians of Canada remember far more poignantly than any other Canadians the heritage of poverty, of bad health, of despair and of early death that the regime represented by that grotesque caricature of a welfare system known as the Indian Act imposed upon them. As for the newcomers, they tend too often to take on the stances of conquerors, intent on keeping what they have taken, in terms of land especially, and clinging to the old stereotypes of idle Indians, comic Eskimos and shifty halfbreeds. They have failed to see, as white Canadians have usually failed, that minorities may have their own ways of existence which are right for them, and that the imposition of majority values is morally indefensible. That great Native person, Louis Riel, addressing the court in Regina as he stood on trial for his life at the end of the 1885 rebellions, put the argument with great clarity.

> I suppose the halfbreeds in Manitoba, in 1870, did not fight for two hundred and forty acres of land, but it is to be understood that there were two societies who treated together. One was small, but in its smallness it had its rights. The other was great, but in greatness it has no greater rights than the rights of the small, because the right of the small is for everyone, and when they began treating the leaders of that small community as outlaws, leaving them without protection, they disorganized that community.

On both sides resentment is compounded by ignorance, for the average Canadian latecomer, whether urban, suburban or rural, knows and desires to know little about the first peoples even when they live close by. The education system begins by encouraging ignorance; recently, researching an article on the role of the first peoples in the curricula of British Columbia public schools, I found a nodding acknowledgement of the presence of Native groups, but certainly no evidence of any effort to lead students into positive consideration of the difficulties of relations between the first and later coming peoples. Only a few teachers with very strong personal interests in Indian art and general culture seem to have gone individually beyond the meagre curriculum.

At the same time, one cannot blame the educational authorities entirely, for there is no wealth available of good nonacademic writing about the first peoples. Ethnologists are either unwilling to share their knowledge with general readers or too crippled by their own pseudo-scientific jargon to do so, though they are very willing to attack nonprofessionals who have ventured into their field, as I know from experience. Up to now the first peoples themselves, advancing slowly into the fields of higher education and into the peripheries of the literary and artistic worlds, have contributed very little to the sum of our knowledge about them; one respects their modesty. We are made aware of their problems by the eloquent and often legally trained activists—Ovide Mercredi a shining example among them—who have risen in recent years into the positions of chiefs and spokesmen, but there are few first people who tell us of the reality of their traditions, the quality of their life at its best, and the embodied wisdom.

The problem of stereotypes held on both sides is paramount. If late Canadians too often see first people as the men and women from the untidy houses of the local reserve who tend to populate prairie prisons or degenerate in the drug-drink-and-prostitution rings on the skid roads of western cities like Vancouver, Winnipeg and Regina, first people on Skid Road and the reserves—the ones who do not escape by way of the law offices—see the rest of us as represented by the Indian Affairs bureaucrats, the C-grade teachers and the mounted police, who batten on them, mock them, bully them, sometimes assault them and generally keep them in their position as Welfare State wards.

The mere breaking down of stereotypes is one of the major tasks we face, particularly as new stereotypes replace the old and discredited ones. Recently there have been many media items—films, television shows, magazine articles, books—that portray the first peoples as mainly the passive victims of physical deprivation and mental anomie. Unrelieved by material of a more positive cast that might stress the cultural and political resurgence of the first peoples in recent years, such efforts result in the creation of a new stereotype. The ferocious Indian of long ago and the idle and untrustworthy Indian of more recent years have been replaced by the contemporary Indian as victim. The unfortunate effect of stereotyping is that it changes the way people look at themselves as well as the way other people look at them. Nowadays I encounter well-educated and prosperous first people who have attained good positions in the "white" world, imagining and presenting themselves as victims when they should be encouraging their people to be victors in the struggle to realize their own values and utilize them posi- tively, within their own communities and within a Canada where people will understand each other even if they are not united. Unity, in any case, is no more than a phantasm echoing in the empty heads of politicians. The natural state of relations between human beings and human communities is mutualist, and this the traditions of the first peoples teach us.

IV

WHILE IT MAY TAKE A GREAT DEAL of patient intercourse and discussion before we can find to the full degree what the first peoples can contribute to a new Canada, we can already begin to see the main directions of enquiry, which should not be delayed, since without the understanding such an enquiry can bring we shall never evolve a political arrangement that will satisfy all the communities within Canada.

What we see, looking at such history of the first peoples as we have, is a pattern of unstructured societies (groups of extended families) developing into lightly structured polities (bands, tribes, confederations). And I perceive a number of general characteristics in these transitional structures that have been evident during the period since the latecomers began recording them. They tend to be consensual and libertarian, with authority generally temporary and linked to expertise or more fragilely to prestige. They tend to be decentralist and to favour confederal patterns rather than nation-statist ones when units larger than the band do emerge in tentative unification. They are inclined economically toward what is often called "primitive communism," the sharing in accordance with long traditions of mutual aid of the animals killed in the hunt, of fish catches, of the produce of fields worked or berry patches picked over by the clan. And, finally, in general their societies have not been static and unchanging.

Already, when the European explorers and traders arrived there were Indian peoples who had passed beyond the primal loose arrangement of families into bands, developing tribes out of bands sharing languages and eventually creating confederations that, in the case of the Blackfoot, went beyond linguistic unity by admitting the Athapaskan-speaking Sarcee. But this steady expansion of the active political units from family to band to tribe to confederation did not mean nation-making in the European sense. The council of sachems of the Iroquois League of Five Nations (which eventually became six) had no authority over the internal affairs of the tribes; it was a body for deciding the common interests of the peoples of the league and for agreeing by consensus, if that were possible, on common action. If no consensus was reached, no common action was taken, although this did not prevent the war chiefs of the individual tribes from calling their supporters together for a raid, so that many of the actions in the so-called Iroquois wars were carried out by individual tribes, usually either the Seneca or the Mohawk, which had the strongest military traditions and the strongest warrior societies.

The talk of war brings one to the main criticism made of the traditional Native societies: that while they were indeed expanding and become more inclusive without developing authoritarian political structures, warriors were influential and respected among them, war was one of the ways—beside eloquence and hunting skills—for a man to realize and establish himself, and hostility to the stranger seems to have been almost a general rule. Enmities between groups could be visceral in their intensity, as between the Inuit and the tribes to the south of them, resulting occasionally in appalling massacres like that which Samuel Hearne witnessed but could not halt, when in the eighteenth century he accompanied a band of Chipewyan to the mouth of the Coppermine River and they chanced upon a defenceless group of Inuit. Slave raids were frequent among the tribes of the Pacific coast, and no stranger was safe in a village there unless he had the protection of an important household; slaves were regarded as chattels over whom the owners had power of life and death; at the extravagant potlatches of the mid-nineteenth century, the chiefs would sometimes kill slaves in the same way as they burnt elaborately carved canoes, just to show their contempt for the wealth they displayed on behalf of their clans. And the cruelty with which the Iroquois sometimes tortured to death their captured enemies received ample attention in missionary accounts, in the narratives of European and American historians, and in popular novels.

In fact, there are several appropriate answers to the argument relating to the warlike nature of the societies developed by the first peoples. It is true that in the barren North there was endemic war even among the least organized groups, caused largely by competition for scanty and unpredictable game resources, although evasion seems to have been as frequent a practice as combat. It was smallpox rather than warfare that radically reduced the population of all the Americas in the late eighteenth and early nineteenth centuries. At the same time, historians do not so widely stress that from ancient prehistoric times there was extensive trading not only between neighbouring tribes and bands, but also over routes that might stretch across half the continent and by which commodities like eulachon grease from the Nass River, obsidian from the Chilcotin area, dentalium shell from Vancouver Island, pemmican from the prairies, native copper from Lake Superior and Alaska, and the wampum of the Atlantic coast penetrated into distant places. Trade routes and traders seem to have operated under rules of sacredness or taboo like those that protected the roads to Olympia or Delphi when the Games were held, or the rivermouth markets of the Solomon Islands where the mutually hostile bush peoples and coast peoples come together to this day to exchange their products. Certain lineages among the Tlingit and the Tsimshian (otherwise warlike peoples) maintained complex trading links with the interior Athapaskan bands. All along the Pacific coast from Alaska to northern California a trading pidgin was used that was actually a simplified version of Chinook, the language of a powerful trading tribe settled around the mouth of the Columbia and particularly active in the great seasonal markets at the Dalles, which attracted people from both the coastal rain forest and the dry interior plateau.

Apart from the presence of trade as a counterbalance to warfare among the first peoples, one must take into account both the circumstances in which the Europeans saw "Indian cruelty" and the interests of those who reported it. The politics of the Catholic church made the Jesuits, who were resented by the older missionary orders, anxious to establish a martyrology that would be the basis of a hagiolatry, and it suited them to be seen serving God among a swarm of sadistic savages. And both the English and the French found it convenient to make the most of whatever atrocities were perpetuated by the Native auxiliaries of the other side. The sacrificial killing by torture of captured warriors did indeed take place, but there were always some who were spared to be adopted into the tribe, including a substantial number of French Canadian captives. By the end of the eighteenth century, in fact, the Iroquois bands had become so deprived of manpower by their incessant warfare that they were adopting captives by the score, and it is generally considered that the Six Nations, by the time they came to Canada at the end of the American revolutionary war in 1783, contained only a tiny proportion of pure-blood Iroquois. Apart from that there were Indian peoples like the Ojibwa and Native chiefs like the great Tecumseh, who entirely rejected the practice of sacrificial torture killings.

Nor can one ignore the extent to which the arrival of the Europeans exacerbated the pattern of small-scale raiding that was endemic in the life of the first peoples. Even the men of God carried a message of war rather than of peace, for French priests were active in organizing the Micmacs of what is now Nova Scotia and New Brunswick to attack New England communities. Colonial governors and military commanders developed a powerful weapon of terrorism in encouraging the excesses of their Native auxiliaries. And the traders, whether they were the Dutch on the Hudson River, or the English on Hudson's Bay, or the French operating from the St. Lawrence, profoundly changed the balance of Native societies by selling firearms. The mobility and the power to surprise introduced by the horse and the gun changed bands of timid foot hunters into bold warriors with their own codes of military honour. Seeking new sources of furs to trade, the Cree and other peoples near Hudson's Bay used their advantage in weapons to sweep over the northern parkland region, and a whole section of the Cree, the Plains Cree, formed an alliance with the Siouan-speaking Assiniboine (or Stonies) whose members adopted the expansive bison-hunting lifestyle, pushed the Blackfoot into the western plains and drove the Gros Ventres out of Canada.

Yet this warlike culture, like the similarly military culture of the Iroquois, remained obstinately unauthoritarian. The chiefs who often seemed to Europeans to hold so much power were hardly rulers at all in the true sense; early missionary observers constantly note how precarious their influence was. Although heredity might enter into the process through the son of a capable father having a name to start with, chiefs were in the main chosen for their personal qualities—wisdom, ability, eloquence—and their peers, the best hunters and warriors and orators, generally chose them by consensus. They did not give orders, since these would have been disobeyed; they argued and persuaded, and when their suggestions were unanimously adopted, after open discussion, it was because they were good, rather than because they emanated from the chief.

A kind of negative mechanism of recall existed, since a chief who failed to maintain the respect of his fellows or whose advice led the tribe into difficulty would soon find his support leaching away. A further corrective to power-seeking on the part of the chiefs lay in the warriors' societies that existed among the politically most highly organized groups, the Blackfoot and the Iroquois, and also in bison hunting tribes like the Plains Cree and the Assiniboine. In most tribes, everywhere in Canada, the military organization was separate from the civil organization, rather as the knightly orders like the Templars or the Teutonic Knights maintained their own structures and their right to independent action at least for a period in medieval Europe. At certain times the warriors of the military societies would take over, particularly during the great collective bison hunts; they would not only police the camps, but would also determine the line of march and administer the rules of the hunt, which were framed in such a way that no individual should gain advantage over the rest or disturb the bison herd before the signal had been given for a general assault.

The most sophisticated organization of the bison hunt was developed by the Red River Métis from Cree practice. As many as four hundred hunters might take part, with women and children accompanying them to process the hides and sun-dry the meat or turn it into pemmican. On the first day out from Red River, the hunters would gather to elect their leader, their guide and the captains, who would see to the maintenance of discipline, and the making, watching and defending of camps against the rival Dakota Sioux hunters. This was always a temporary arrangement, lasting only until the Métis column was on the way home, far from the herds and out of danger from the Dakota, and though leaders like Gabriel Dumont might be chosen in successive years because of their experience as marksmen and hunters, they retained no authority over the wandering Métis camps between the periodic hunts.

Except—and it is a very significant exception in view of later demands by the first peoples for self-government—the instance of St. Laurent on the South Saskatchewan River. There, recognizing that the bison were vanishing and encouraged by the Oblate missionary, Father André, Dumont and his fellow hunters set up in 1873 a commune—a people's republic—that was the first attempt at municipal organization in the Northwest Territories. The commune, administered by a council chosen in a public meeting by discussion and consensus, with Dumont as president, established sets of rules designed—too late, unfortunately—to conserve the bison herds, but also to regulate such matters as land holding and timber rights that related to the new status of the Métis as unwillingly settled people. The commune appears to have worked very well, until Dumont and his captains intercepted some hunters employed by the Hudson's Bay Company who were breaking the rules laid down for the buffalo hunt by the St. Laurent people, and confiscated their equipment as a fine. This brought them up against both the old and the new powers in the yet unorganized territory, the Company and the North-West Mounted Police. While admitting that André and Dumont had created a kind of order where none existed, the Mounted Police nevertheless forced the dissolution of the commune. (The Métis took their revenge at Duck Lake in 1885.)

Thus, among the prairie tribes and to an extent among the Métis there was really a dual pattern of administration, with the chief or leader and his advisors operating at ordinary times through argument and example, and also through custom as remembered by the elders (but not through laws, which are an invention of the literate) and at exceptional times through warriors' or hunters' societies operating with a degree of discipline that involved customary punishments during special operations such as warfare and the collective hunt; nobody was forced to take part in any such operation, but once committed, they had to follow the rules that war chiefs or experienced hunters might enforce.

Among the Iroquois, a third force interestingly appeared, that of the women. It is true that there have been women chiefs among certain tribes in the Pacific Northwest and in northern Canada; today the chief of the Musqueam Salish, just down the road from my home, is a very capable woman (one of a succession), and the most notable chief of the Chilliwack Salish in recent years was a Norwegian woman who had married a former chief and thus acquired "Indian status." But generally the position of the women has been functionally subordinate; they performed the menial jobs while the men gained glory as hunters and warriors.

The Iroquois were exceptional as the most thoroughly agrarian group of first peoples in Canada, and among them the women played a crucial role as cultivators and processors of the principal resources—corn and beans, squash and sunflowers. In addition, Iroquois were matrilineal and matrilocal, if not strictly matriarchal, so that succession and inheritance ran through the female lines of the clans possessing longhouses, and in the longhouses the women made the decisions, since the men were only guests. The women had their own secret societies which paralleled the men's military societies, but their secrets were well kept, and the actual power of the women has been much debated, although the role of the longhouse mothers in the recent Oka crisis suggests that it was considerable. However this may be, Iroquois women certainly played one central role in traditional government. The federal council of the League of Five—and later Six—nations was administered (ruled would be too strong a word) by a council of fifty sachems. These were picked from fifty longhouses, equivalent to matrilineal lineages, among the various tribes from the Seneca in the West to the Mohawk in the East, and each was chosen—in consultation with the other women of the clan—by the senior matron of the longhouse.

There was an interesting provision for recall in this arrangement, in the case of a chief failing to meet his responsibility as representative of his clan with dignity and diligence. The clan mother, accompanied by the war chief of the clan, would pay a call on him, and never would he fail to resign, knowing that tribal public opinion would be on the side of his critics. Thus women, warriors and wise men were intimately associated in Iroquois public life, and a useless politician had a shorter active life than he might have in our parliamentary system.

As I have been considering and writing this essay, I have become steadily more convinced that I am not dealing with a series of static tribal polities belonging to the past. The political genius of the first peoples lies largely in adaptability. One of the developments that has most impressed me in recent years is the demonstration of the political capabilities of groups of first people who less than a generation ago were organized in the simple and basic manner of family groups wandering over the harsh northland with so little law and political organization that they once delighted anarchist theoreticians with their examples of developing sophisticated technologies of physical survival while neglecting anything political. The Inuit especially, and the Athapaskan bands that now insist on calling themselves Dené, lived for centuries and doubtless for millennia as wandering hunters, who very occasionally would meet people speaking the same language on some hunt or fishing expedition, but who directed all their collective genius into devising the ultimate in Stone Age techniques to feed and clothe themselves in one of the world's most rigorous environments. Yet in recent years, these very denizens of the North, with their vestigial political structures, have come together in some of the most effective voluntary organizations among the first peoples, the Dené Nation and the Inuit Taparisat, which have fought effectively on such matters of common interest as land claims and the self-government of the first peoples, and have sustained the communalism essential to their past role as hunters in their tendency to apply collectively whatever wealth in land or cash they gain from agreements with the latecoming communities.

V

MORE THAN A CENTURY AGO, in the 1860s on the eve of the foundation of the First International, the French political philosopher Pierre Joseph Proudhon wrote an influential book entitled *The Political Capabilities of the Working Class*, showing how workers were capable of managing their own affairs without the interference of leaders from other classes. It is now time somebody wrote a new book, *The Political Capabilities of the First Peoples of Canada*, showing how much flexibility and wisdom our firstcomers have shown in managing their own affairs where they have had the necessary basis in resources. You may not find such capabilities flourishing in some isolated reserve with little communication, no resource base, half the people sick, and 90 percent on welfare. But put such people in a situation where there is hope and a chance of helping themselves, and the prospects change immediately. These are people from whom we must learn in changing our own imperfect structures, and that is why I see the process of constitution-making—in so far as we need anything so rigid as a constitution—as a process of learning and understanding on all sides. The fur traders took the first peoples as mentors in penetrating the land through ancient technologies of canoe, sled and snowshoe; we must take them as our mentors in the essentials of social organization. We have much to teach each other.

If one could imagine a joint constitutional assembly or council of firstcomers and latecomers taking place in Canada, what might be the most fruitful areas of discussion? I can think of four of them. The first, as the last essay suggests, relates to leadership; do we want guidance and good opinion by good people with no presumption to direction, which is the Native view of leadership? Or do we want the charismatic but usually unwise party leader instructing his followers and, ultimately, an unwilling populace? Our problem is not to find people who will magically do things for us, but people who will guide us into making up our minds wisely without taking responsibility away from us. Here, the nonauthoritarian concept of chiefship is far superior to any style of leadership we have developed.

Naturally, the question of leadership leads us to the fact that the loose structure of chiefs with prestige but no active authority, arguing points in council and assembly until everyone more or less agrees, in the customary Native way, is in sharp contrast to the pyramidical structure of authority and obedience which is the latecomer Canadian norm. The advocates of that form of representative democracy argue that it is necessary for long-term policies. But Native peoples are much more concerned with immediate and local questions of survival, land, sovereignty, preserving traditional values; and in the modern world survival has become a prime desideratum. Communication with Native people may teach us how to make our own system less rigid, more responsive to the never constant will of the people, and to their needs, better geared to the rapid pace of change in our century, to the urgency of matters of environment, and hence of survival, that affect us all.

This brings us to the kind of reconstruction needed if we are intent on building a horizontal rather than a vertical democracy. The citizen has to face that he is permanently a part of the decision-making body, and that sovereignty begins not with any collectivity but with the individual. Rare western countries like Switzerland are organized so that, through various devices, the voice of the citizen can be heard often and at many levels. In Canada, the tendency of Native peoples to create temporary ad hoc structures (like the smoothly running councils of the buffalo hunt and the involvement of some in naming and recalling chiefs among the Iroquois) set us examples worth exploring in new contexts. So does the ability, shown by the Dené and the Inuit, to create—virtually out of nothing—effective political structures on the consensual model rather than that of the majoritarian democracy, which in practice turns out to be authoritarian. We have many useful lessons to learn, if we will only put aside the pride of our parliamentary traditions and listen to other voices and experiences.

Finally, there is the question of an effective replacement for the Welfare State and the dependent mentality bred by welfare practices. Among us, welfare has become the mechanism of a society that once used churchly charity to mask its essential inequalities. Its worst result is probably to destroy the natural forces of mutual aid that exist in every true society. The Native peoples began with survival rather than charity. When there was food in the clan, it must be distributed effectively to all those who needed to eat, without distinction. Long before European socialists, the Native peoples developed in practice the central idea of what Kropotkin called "Mutual Aid": "From each according to his means, to each according to his need." When Gabriel Dumont, as leader of the buffalo hunt, rode through the herd again and again to kill more bison which he gave to the old and disabled, the sick and the orphaned, it was not out of Christian charity; it was from urges of tribal solidarity inherited from his Indian ancestors.

The Native peoples know a great deal about the Welfare State and its systems; in fact, it began in Canada with the various Indian Acts and the agencies set up to administer them. It has grown since then into a great many-armed monster like the legendary Kraken. Perhaps the wisdom and the aid of the Native peoples will help us to replace it with the revival of the voluntary mutual aid institutions and impulses that are proper to free and healthy societies.

4

MENDING A FRAGMENTED FATHERLAND

The fatherland, for us, is the whole of Canada, that is the federation of distinct races and provinces. The nation which we wish to see developed is the Canadian nation, composed of French Canadians and English Canadians, that is to say, two elements separated by language and religion, and by the legal arrangements necessary for the conservation of their respective traditions, but united in an attachment to brotherhood, in a common attachment to a common fatherland.

— Henri Bourassa, 1904

I

SO SPOKE, ALMOST NINETY YEARS AGO, one of the greatest and purest-hearted advocates of an autonomous role for Québec within a Canadian confederation. Henri Bourassa was no relative of the current premier of Québec, but he was a predecessor less spoilt by the life of politics. He was hardly a separatist in the modern sense, and his all-Canadian patriotism was perhaps of a more genuine kind than that of many Anglophone conservatives of his day who still, in the first decade of the twentieth century, upheld militantly imperialist doctrines. They envisaged Canada not as a true sovereign country but as an increasingly equal partner in an empire dominated by a consortium of white races, with French Canadians and Afrikaners somewhat condescendingly allowed to play their parts beside the British. Since Bourassa saw Canada as a North American nation that had ceased to owe anything to its parent polities, either Britain or France, it seemed logical—and patriotic—for him to oppose Canada's entry into World War One, as he had already opposed its entanglement in the Boer War, and to take the Québecois side in the conscription dispute that would be one of the earliest of the wrenching struggles between English- and French-speaking peoples in Canada.

Though he first disputed the terms of the relationship, Henri Bourassa was devoted to the basic *idea* of Canada, the confederationist pattern of peoples living together and showing to the world examples of intercultural harmony and the kind of freedom from imperial domination that a country like Canada might achieve without becoming a homogenous nation-state. Both Bourassas—almost a century apart—talked of "distinct societies," and if one had to define the differences between the older and the younger, one could cite perhaps the steady leaching away of trust between the French and English from its peak in Laurier's day. An even greater difference is the increasing professionalization of Canadian politics which has accompanied the narrowing, in recent years, of the gap between the "two solitudes" in terms of mutual awareness between Anglophones and Francophones.

This change in climate of political relations offers the reason why we should, at the risk of appearing churlishly intransigent, reject the proposals of Bourassa and his government for the recognition of *Québec alone* as a distinct society, and stand out for the recognition of all Canadian regional societies as equally distinct. I distrusted the proposal from the beginning, since the narrow provincial chauvinism of Québec's language policies had appalled me, and it seemed to me that the Native peoples of Ungava, as they themselves fear, would probably be worse off under the bureaucrats of an independent Québec than they now are under federal Indian Affairs officials. But I decided finally against the Québec proposals when British Columbia Premier William Vander Zalm proposed that the simplest thing would be to declare all the regions of Canada distinct societies.

The since discredited Vander Zalm was foolish in his handling of the patronage that is the lifeblood of Canadian politics, and even more foolish in handling the personal wealth he gathered with such a natural ease. But he sometimes showed the genuine simple man's insights one would expect of a good gardener, and he was right about the regions of Canada all being viable distinct societies.

I shall enlarge later on the general implications of this suggestion. The immediate point is that the reaction of the Québecois *and* the federal politicians to this just and simple proposal revealed how far the issue affected what federal and provincial politicians saw as their legitimate powers, and how much it had become a hard political bargaining point unrelated to the cultures of Canada or to the interests of ordinary Canadians. Bourassa bristled arrogantly at Vander Zalm's proposal, accusing him of insultingly trivializing a matter of deep seriousness to the Québecois. The rest of the political herd skirted around the problem as if the idea of a group of strong and distinct regional identities revealing themselves in English-speaking Canada were a naïve fantasy; such identities, of course, exist.

But politicians on both sides of the language fence chose to ignore this reality and to use the traditional distrust between the "two solitudes" to create two homogenous unilingual power blocs, in which the "distinctness" of Québec will be used to prevent its people from ever making common cause with other Canadians. The idea is ultimately unworkable, but it may be sustained for a while to keep power from filtering into the lower levels of society, which has been one of the prime aims of both federal and provincial politicians.

The "distinct society" of Québec alone will be a failure from the beginning. It will not even contain all the French-speaking people of Canada, for the Acadians will not want to join the Québecois, and the French-speaking people of the West will be able to do so only by migration. Québec itself will resemble one of those unstable republics set up in Europe after World War One and the collapse of the Dual Monarchy, for it will be forced into the process of appeasing dangerous minorities of second-class citizens—English, Jewish, European immigrants who incline toward Anglophone values and increasingly militant aboriginal groups.

Homogenous English Canada, from Newfoundland to British Columbia, which the centralists who call themselves "federalists" promote, is projected as a union of Anglophones in which bilingualism will flow quietly away like the bathwater as a semblance of multiculturalism is cultivated to placate the non-English groups who will make up more than 40 percent of the population of such a non-French rump of Canada. Such a homogenous English Canada exists only in the minds of politicians for whom the country's future depends on the manipulation of language blocs.

II

THERE IS IN FACT no single English Canada, just as there is no single French one. For language is not the only or even the principal element that makes a distinct society; it is not even a necessarily divisive element, for there are countries like Switzerland that have more official languages than Canada, and some, like India, that have many more and yet survive. This they do by recognizing their diversities and building on them.

Canadian regions are sharply defined by history, by geography, by economic function. They were settled at different times and in different circumstances. Newfoundland began in the annual fishing expeditions from Europe, and continued in the anarchic order of the Masterless Men. British Columbia was opened to the European world by the fur traders, whom the gold-seekers pushed aside in the mid-nineteenth century. Ontario and Montreal were largely populated by people fleeing the Irish potato famines of the 1840s, and the prairies by Slavic peoples who escaped Russian and Austrian tyrannies late in the nineteenth century. The Maritime provinces other than Newfoundland were settled through a filtration from the American colonies, which intensified when the great flood of loyalists in the 1780s led to the foundation of New Brunswick.

Not only were the provinces settled at sharply different times, from the early sixteenth century in Newfoundland to the mid-nineteenth century in British Columbia, and the turn of the century on the prairies; most of them also entered the confederation of Canada as already autonomous entities within the British Empire. As we have seen, confederation took place in 1867 when the appropriate legislation was passed by the British Parliament *at the request* of the British North American provinces, which by that very request declared their existing sovereignty. But New Brunswick and Nova Scotia had second thoughts and might have withdrawn in 1867 if the Imperial government had not shown itself disinclined to repeal the BNA.

British Columbia did not enter until 1871, and then with misgivings and continued threats of secession that went on until the early 1880s, because the federal government tried to back down on its promise of a transcontinental railway, offered as bait to ensure the entry of the far western province. Prince Edward Island also came in because of railway politics, having built an island system for which it could not pay. Manitoba—a mere fragment of its present extent—entered at the end of the long period of resistance to Canadian rule known as the Red River Rebellion of 1870. Newfoundland only came in, bankrupt and resentful, in 1945, seventy-eight years after the original confederation, and then only by a tiny minority on a referendum. Only the two remaining prairie provinces, Saskatchewan and Alberta, were created by fiat of the federal government, but they too came into Canada under special circumstances, the sudden and rapid population of the prairies by an unprecedented mixture of peoples from the 1880s onwards. Like the northern territories, with their majority of aboriginal peoples, they form an area where the majority of the inhabitants belong to traditions other than English or French. So much for the myth of an English bloc consisting of two-thirds of the people of Canada! As we see, all the six parts of "English" Canada which we count as its regions—Newfoundland, the Maritimes, Ontario, the prairie West, British Columbia, and the northern territories—have sharply separate histories, and the majority of them were autonomous political entities before they became part of the confederation. They are as distinct from each other as Québec is from each of them individually, and only the fact that French is the language spoken by most (but not all) of the people in Québec remains as a unique sign of distinction.

For the other cultural elements that might have been regarded as distinguishing Québec have in fact diminished over the past century. Henri Bourassa could call on the special role of the church and religion in Québec life, but the Quiet Revolution of the 1960s undermined all that vast ecclesiastical influence and pushed the foot of the priest outside the door of the house. Education, health services, a great deal of welfare, were taken out of the hands of the religious orders and turned over to secular agencies. Thus the church in Québec has retreated into its sacerdotal role, and, considered merely on a religious basis, it is in essence no different from the Catholicism of the millions of Irish, Poles, Italians, Portuguese or south Germans who attend the churches of the old faith in the rest of Canada.

It is true that in recent decades, literature and the visual arts flourished in Québec, and have been supported by nationalistically inclined governments. But surprisingly little of the literature breaks out toward the dialect forms like joual that are peculiar to Québec and Acadia. In fact, just as Canadian literature in English seems to stand as the younger cousin in the family of English literatures, and the writer awaits an ultimate accolade from London or New York, so has Québecois writing in recent years increasingly oriented itself toward Paris for its models and its medals. Similarly, Québec painters in the twentieth century have consistently found their inspiration in the metropolitan art scene of Paris. As in the case of Canadian writing in English, the intense nationalism of the 1960s and early 1970s has long died away as a motivating force among Québecois writers, whose essential aims and achievements, like those of writers in English or Icelandic or Ukrainian or Iroquois, is to honour the life and the land they know, which in each case is a regionally limited territory with its own human culture.

On the popular level, the situation is not much different. Everywhere in Canada, whatever the language spoken, ice hockey is the game followed with most passion, television takes its examples from south of the border, locally produced films show interests as narrow and refined as their audiences, and on the *patate frite* level, popular fun and pleasure are much as they are among the hot dogs.

So, remembering how much the traditions of the English and the French in Canada come together, in their phases of fishing and fur trading, of farming and eventually industry, of Indian wars merging into wars with each other, of periods of resentful isolation from each other alternating with periods of surprising cordiality, we have to recognize that we could all share the nostalgic dream, "je me souviens," and that the historic reasons for mutual resentment are as insubstantial as the reasons for all the other mass hatreds: French versus English, German versus French, Poles versus Russians, Mexicans versus gringos, Inuit versus Indians. True, a generation of English long ago conquered a generation of Québecois, yet in the process they liberated them from an autocratic monarchy and gave them a democratic system they have used ever since. As for Confederation, there the Upper and Lower Canadians appeared as the double victors; so far as the Maritimers and the peoples of the various Wests were concerned, it acted as a kind of conquest without arms, subjecting them, from the inception of Macdonald's National Policy in 1879, consistently to the interests of Ontario and Québec, as it still does.

III

IN EFFECT, THE CONCLUSION WE MUST REACH is that language, which Québecois ideologues indeed regard as the substantial and symbolic issue between them and their neighbours, is in effect the only factor that can perhaps make Québec society more distinct—more "pas comme les autres" as we used to say—than the broadly differing regions of "English Canada." But the relation of a separate language to a national tradition is a more complex one than it appears to many in Canada today. Let me make a few proposals.

1. Profound national traditions and loyalties do not in fact demand the presence of a still vigorous original language on the part of the insurgent nationality. Of the four Celtic nations (Scots, Irish, Welsh, Cornish) still embraced at the beginning of this century in the United Kingdom, Wales had—and still has—the highest proportion of people speaking the Celtic language, but it was Ireland, where Gaelic was spoken by a small minority, that kept up a long and eventually effective resistance to the English. Most Irish still habitually speak English, and they have contributed nobly to modern English literature. English is also, despite all efforts to dislodge it, the working common language of multilingual India. Yet neither country is other than distinct and independent.

2. Even for the Québecois, language is not an irrevocable bond, for in two successive world wars the people of the province refused to accept that sharing a language with the French might oblige them to take part in two wars aimed at liberating their mother country from German aggression and occupation.

3. A language is only of value as the characteristic of a people if it is spoken freely; to impose it by law, as various Québecois governments have attempted, merely makes it an artificial rule forced on the unwilling, and therefore inherently fragile. Only if it is voluntarily accepted is a language a legitimate mark of distinctness.

4. Switzerland has not one but *four* officially recognized languages; it has no official policy of quadrilingualism, nor does any of the Cantons-, German-, French- or Italian-speaking, or the scattered communities that speak Romansch, attempt to impose in any way the use of the locally dominant language. To the contrary, the Swiss are proud of their ethnic and linguistic diversity, so that in 1938 they voted overwhelmingly in favour of a referendum that gave official status to Romansch, spoken by one percent of the confederation's population, living in some remote communes of the Grisons. Compared with such fair-minded magnanimity, the attempts of Québec nationalists of all shades to impose their language on those residents of the province who prefer not to use it, seems petty and tyrannical; there is something disconcertingly craven about their argument that their culture will die out if their language is not protected by strict laws. Great, proud, self-confident cultures do not behave in this way, like children frightened by the dark of change. Québecois chauvinist leaders, like most politicians, neglect to read history, which would teach them that languages survive because people have uses for them, and only decline when they become irrelevant to the way of life to which they have given expression in the past.

To sum up, I believe that the distinctness of Canada's regional cultures is an important one, because it provides the only basis on which we can effectively remake and revitalize our confederation. But for that revitalization to happen, every region of Canada must increase its degree of self-government (as the Native cultures must do at the same time), and this can only happen if they are all, simultaneously, recognized as distinct societies. There is nothing insulting to Québecois hopes in such a statement; indeed, it would be more insulting to assume that Québec's regional culture is so weak that it demands the protection of a unique and special status. And it must be obvious to anyone seeking a lasting solution to the problems of Canadian peoples that granting the status of a distinct society to Québec alone, especially if it is accompanied by the granting of constitutional vetoes, will lock us into the situation of two homogenous monoliths, French Canada and English Canada, the very nemesis from which we have been trying to escape. Our negotiators should acquire some of the skills of the Asian bazaar, including that of walking away, with dramatic contempt and arrogance, if the demands of the other side impinge on one's welfare. For even if Ontario is able to accommodate itself to a privileged Québec (which I doubt), neither the prairie West nor British Columbia nor the Atlantic provinces can do so if it interferes with the urgent task of reconstructing the regional arrangements of Canada.

IV

WHEN I TALK OF REGIONAL ARRANGEMENTS, it must be clear that I am evoking something different from the narrow provincial self-interest that Mel Hurtig conceived when he wrote in *The Betrayal of Canada* that "Selfish, self-centred, petty and power hungry provincial potentates, with visions that extend no farther than the steps of contemporary legislatures, are a contemporary plague." I would disagree with Hurtig only to emphasize that greed and power hunger and pettiness are characteristics shared by federal politicians as well. It is a sickness that has been encouraged by the very existence of a constitutional document, the BNA, which was designed to define the powers of two different layers of government, but which has involved us in little better than a constant process of snatching at power, so that certain groups of politicians may gain temporary advantages and enjoy the increase of authority even when they do not gain materially. For corruption, alas, assumes many forms.

The recognition of regions as natural units within which co-operation may flourish is, I suggest, the beginning of an approach to political arrangement directed by geographical and social realities and aimed at the benefit of the people as groups and individuals. The original provinces of Canada were marked off as colonies for the convenience of imperial administrators. And so regions essentially differ from provinces in the sense that they are physical terrains with natural boundaries, containing separate economies and ecologies, and inhabited by distinct combinations of people who share common histories.

Sometimes a province and a region coincide, as in the cases of Newfoundland, isolated by the sea, and British Columbia, isolated by its ranges of mountains, each with its very individual history before entering Canada. But very often the provinces are merely the misconceived creations of those men so influential in shaping modern North America, the surveyors whose straight lines ride across the prairies and the parklands without natural diversion and without regard for the regional realities that are divided in this way. For the West, from the Canadian Shield to the foothills of the Rockies, is a slowly changing geographical unity, now largely devoted to the most destructive forms of cash-based monoculture. For centuries, Native peoples wandered as nomads over its surface, following the great bison herds that acknowledged no frontiers; all three prairie provinces formed the battlefields of the great fur companies in the early nineteenth century, and later they became the destination of the thousands of poor but hardy peasant farmers who came from the subject territories of the great central European empires. Thus, the three prairie provinces, despite their political division, are united by geography and tradition into a single region with shared interests, shared problems (notably how to emerge from limited economies). In the same way, the three maritime provinces retain in common not only much of their past history, but also the chronic state of lasting economic depression that has resulted from the miscarriage of confederation as a possible solution for their problems. History and language separate Québec, as well as the fact that it is essentially concentrated toward the valley of the St. Lawrence, Canada's original great artery, while, apart from always having seen itself as the bastion of British culture in Canada (which other provinces would undoubtedly dispute), Ontario is indubitably shaped by the fact that except for its rocky pre-Cambrian hinterland, it is the land of the Great Lakes, the world's largest areas of varyingly polluted fresh water, which have always provided a special entry into the heart of the continent.

It is these country-sized regions that might well be the essential units of a truly confederalist and decentralized Canada. The basic idea of confederalism, or of real federalism for that matter, is that the people in general know best how to manage their own affairs, and should be allowed to do so as long as they do not harm the welfare of their fellow citizens. Small communities should have entire control over everything that is of interest only to their inhabitants—basic freedoms and rights being taken for granted. Certainly we should bring an end to anomalous situations where the federal and provincial governments dispute authority in the same fields, as they do in British Columbia, where there are conflicts over fishing and forestry and even the management of wildlife.

The extent to which the confusion among various authorities occurs can be shown when the federal fishery bureaucracy complains because a provincial forestry bureaucracy is allowing clearcut logging beside spawning streams, in the process polluting them; at the same time, both of these authorities override local communities. A recent incident especially angered both local environmentalists and advocates of effective local government. The Surrey, British Columbia council passed a bylaw prohibiting hunting in the municipality; it had the support of most of the local population. But a representative of the federal Wildlife Branch stood up to inform the council that such a bylaw—which referred only to municipal territory—was beyond their competence. All the local authority might possibly do was to pass a bylaw that limited hunting on the grounds of safety. And if the councillors should be presumptuous enough to take this course, the federal government would fight them all the way up through the courts. Only a confederational structure that recognizes—on a widening and rising grade of application—the right and responsibility of communities and local populations to manage their own affairs will produce a society that effectively reflects the trends, perceptions and dwindling resources of the late twentieth century.

At present we have a system, sanctified by an imperfect constitution, that vests authority in the federal and the provincial governments, which in their turn are operated by political party machines mainly concerned with seizing and holding power. In order to open up the rigidities of the system, and to empower the people to the fullest possible degree, we need—I am suggesting—a complication of the structure which in the end will lead to a withering of government and to a much more natural order of administration.

Even when the boundaries of a region and a province coincide, there should be a regional council separate from the provincial government. The function of such a regional council would not be political, but economic, environmental and social. It would deal with resources, including wildlife and its habitat, with the processing of resources and the balancing of economies, with industrial practices, and with the well-being of men, women and children, who have somewhat brutally been termed "human resources." The provincial government would deal with political affairs, and would relate to the federal government in areas of common concern to the country, like transport and communications, foreign relations, customs and excise (if such absurdities survive) the dwindling matter of defence, and how the presently armed forces might be turned into mobile environmental units capable of dealing with disasters in any place and of any size. (My seventh essay deals further with the need to establish Canada as a neutral zone.)

I would suggest that the new regional councils might offer opportunities to explore alternatives to our current political patterns. Elections might be partially direct and partially indirect, a portion of the members being elected at the same time as municipal councils and a portion selected by those councils out of men and women with special knowledge of the region. To avoid the evils of power-playing, nobody who has been an MP or an MLA should be eligible for the regional councils, which essentially would represent the "politics of the unpolitical." Terms should be for no more than two years, only once renewable, with a provision for early recall—if necessary—worked into the system.

And here we might come to a solution of that problem— the Senate of Canada—which has so long been the subject of aggrieved and flatulent debate, particularly in the western regions. The familiar demands of prairie political leaders— with less than dramatic support in British Columbia—have been that whatever replaces the present paddock of worn-out politicians and party workers should be equal, elected and effective; the famous "Three Es," to which one might add the notion that it should no longer be considered the willing instrument of the incumbent prime minister.

Effectiveness is the most obviously necessary quality, but the most difficult to shape into a concrete demand. What in fact is this "effectiveness," or the purpose it must project in an actual Senate if we choose to retain a name so darkened by its use in Rome and the United States?

I have already talked of how a body—let us call it the Chamber of the Regions—might be chosen to represent regions and localities, and this would in fact be the replacement for the Senate. It should correct political decision from social, economic and environmental viewpoints; it should protect individuals and communities, no matter how small and eccentric. It should have the power and duty of both veto and initiative, being able to delay an act of Parliament up to a year to investigate the way it might impinge non-politically on citizens and communities. It should, like the Lords in Britain, be empowered and indeed expected to offer legislation and investigation of its own, particularly in its special area of concern, the national environment.

Essentially, the Chamber of the Regions must be regarded as a body representing the people in its relations with authority, and in this direction its territorial composition enters deeply into the question of its effectiveness. The equality demanded by some westerners, with all provinces having the same number of members, may be good among the fifty states south of the border; in Canada the population disproportions between—say—Prince Edward Island and Québec, make the pattern of regional rather than provincial divisions greatly preferable. Here two provisions seem indispensable. The hinterland of Canada—western and eastern— must be assured that the large central provinces of Ontario and Québec, so often and so shamelessly favoured by federal governments, can no longer combine against them, and in a hypothetical 110-member Chamber of the Regions, perhaps no more than 42 members should be assigned to Ontario and Québec together. The Native peoples should be assigned 4 seats, to fill as they wish, in accordance with their proportion of the population; they will ultimately probably gain another 2 of the 4 territorial seats. The four western provinces should share the remaining 60 seats, perhaps with British Columbia taking 15 seats, Prince Edward Island 5, and the remaining four provinces 10 seats each.

V

IN OUR SEARCH FOR A RENEWED CANADA, the perils of utopianism must be avoided at all costs, and especially the perils of creating an ideal constitution that will become "like the laws of the Persians and the Medes, that it be not altered," or like those tables of laws made by ancient Cretan communities that survive intact in the fields, long after the cities that made them and obeyed them have vanished.

A rigid, utopian constitution would be far worse than no constitution at all; that is why any document defining the Canadian polity must from the outset be tentative and endlessly amendable by request of the people in referenda. No group should hold a position so entrenched that it can block the pass to further change. And that is why even friends of Québec—like the present writer—who welcomed as a great Canadian event the election of René Lévesque's first Parti Québécois government twenty years ago, are filled with apprehension. We saw the Québecois cause then as a progressive development, oriented toward its own kind of social democracy in economic terms, and politically placing itself on the side of a wider concept of national and cultural identity than the one Trudeau seemed to project federally after he showed his authoritarian inclinations so dramatically in 1970.

That was two decades ago, and René Lévesque, who perhaps looked clearly into the future when he resigned from political activity, might well have been troubled by the attitude of his successors. (On the other hand, he might not; nationalists are strange, irrational creatures and usually have a poor grasp of individual freedom, as Québec's present political leaders show, concerned as they are with staking out their defensive position at the expense of the liberties of everyone in Canada, including their own fellow Francophones.)

It is to impede rather than to assist such nationalist

manoeuvres, whether on the Ruritanian scale of Québec City or on the continental scale of Ottawa power brokers (intoxicated that they rule in however spidery a fashion the largest "nation on earth"), that we must put emphasis on a flexible, tentative constitution—if we finally decide to have one, with amendability built into every clause.

In this essay I have been doing my best to work out some of the problems that have to be solved before Canada can fulfill its great potentialities as a confederation. One of them is the recognition that Canada is not—and never has been—a nation-state; geography has defeated any such ambition, as it did in Russia. But the province cut by the surveyor's pencil is as absurd an entity as the nation bounded—as Canada is to the south—by equally artificial frontiers. Canada is a *land*—the very word defines the importance of its varied physical nature. It is the vast sweep of prairie and mountain, of tundra and parkland, of outcropping pre-Cambrian rock and seemingly endless water—whose national barriers, rather than any politicians' arrangements, define the regions that are the true foci of Canadian life. Beside the regions, and nearer the earth of life than the provinces (which desperately try to ignore them) are the localities, the communities, from great cosmopolitan entities like Montréal and, increasingly, Toronto and Vancouver, down to the tiny outports that survived Joey Smallwood's centralizing assault in Newfoundland.

In the Swiss confederation, perhaps the truest we have, the localities (or communes, as they call them), which may have no more than a score of citizens, are the basic units of society. But even the communes are not ultimately sovereign among the Swiss. It is the individual citizen who has the last personal voice in defining the community's interests, through the wide use, on cantonal as well as confederational levels, of those direct voice devices—referendum and initiative. Virtually every law of any importance must be approved not only by elected political bodies but also by the vote of individual citizens.

This area of local empowerment and citizen empowerment, like that of regional administration, has been virtually ignored up to now in our constitutional debates, yet it is vital to any prospect of Canada as a community of peoples that will prosper, or even survive.

5

A Forest Survives through its Undergrowth

I

IN DISCUSSING THE CONCERNS OF THIS CHAPTER—the
autonomy of the community, the powers and claims of the
individual, which together form the vital undergrowth of
the polity—we have to recognize that the community and
the individual are not identical. At times, they have been
made to appear so by political necromancy, as happened
during the French Revolution, when the original concerns
of the Encyclopedists for the freedom of the individual were
overwhelmed by the centralist Jacobin preoccupation with
the Republic One and Indivisible. Revolutionary France
picked up from democratic Athens more than two millennia
before the recurrent problem of how free men might be
induced to support each other, and by a supreme irony
negated its primary essential aim of "liberty" by introducing
the conscription of its citizens into "revolutionary" and later
Napoleonic armies, in which the Greek city communities
had preceded them. Even Switzerland, with its extreme

varieties of direct democracy, rejected the ultimate sovereignty of the individual when it devised its citizen army, to which every adult male must belong. At the same time, the Swiss declared their faith in a polity based on trust when they decreed that every potential fighting citizen should keep his rifle (these days presumably an automatic one) in his own house; up to now there has been no revolt of citizens firing their militia weapons down the Bahnhofstrasse in Zurich.

In Canadian terms, the difference between the concept of group freedoms and that of individual and personal liberties has been a recurrent problem as we have moved toward a more pluralist society over the past generation. Québec offers the type case. At the root of the original conflict in the Cité Libre group of the 1950s, the leading intellectual opponents to Maurice Duplessis's Union Nationale government, was the difference between Trudeau's concept of the Québecois as Canadian citizens without qualification (bilingualism would wipe out the differences between them and their neighbours), and the views of René Lévesque and his companions of Québec as a cultural community to which as such the liberties belonged. The fact that, like the Jacobins, Trudeau eventually became a doctrinaire authoritarian, setting his hopes in a "strong central government," is beside the point. For, despite his various aberrations, Trudeau was enough of an old civil libertarian to ensure that the individualist Charter of Rights was included in what now passes among us as a constitution.

And the fact that even the moderate nationalists of Bourassa's provincial Liberal party defied the Charter to impose restrictions on the use of their language by other than Francophones, shows that they were supporting the rights of a community (and especially of a majority within that community) against those of individuals who happened to form a minority.

A similar situation has arisen in relation to Native groups, and particularly those, like the Iroquois of the Six Nations, who regard themselves as sovereign nations only in alliance with Canada and therefore not subject to the laws of any Canadian confederation that might emerge. In a recent statement, a group purporting to represent the Haudenosaunee or Iroquois Confederacy (Six Nations), but perhaps representing mainly the Mohawk, emphatically reject the concept of personal liberties as opposed to communal ones. They say:

> The Charter protects individual rights. Our govern-
> ments and societies are based on our collective rights—our
> clans and our nations. Our law gives us a very different sense
> of the place of the individual in society. It is not that we
> would deny our own people any rights—but that our ways
> of securing those rights are different from Canada's.

I have brought the Native peoples back into the argument at the time when we are discussing the localization of administration within the regions, partly because, in our less rural regions, Native bands form a large proportion of the population, but partly also because the Six Nations state-ment declares to us quite clearly that there can be many forms of democratic arrangement existing within a larger community, some stressing individual and some collective life. All groups do not have to be alike to live in harmony.

II

ONE OF THE GREAT FAILURES of the kind of majoritarian democracy we have inherited from Britain is that it does not allow comfortable room for alternatives. There are groups in Canada other than the Iroquois, including undoubtedly many of the Native peoples, who see their liberties as collective primarily, and who in any case wish to define them in their own ways. One can instance several religious groups like the Hutterites, and especially the Doukhobors, who became victims of persecution a second time over when they migrated to Canada and came up against the rigorously legalistic nineteenth-century Canadian government.

Their case is worth noting briefly because it shows the flawed attitude that Canada in its growing years adopted toward its minorities. The Doukhobors were a Russian sect, pacifist in action and deeply opposed to the state and earthly rule, even if they were not strictly speaking anarchists. They had originally lived a communitarian life, but had backslid somewhat during the nineteenth century. However, at the turn of the century, they were trying to return to communal living, largely through the influence on their religious leader, Peter the Lordly Verigin, of the writings of Leo Tolstoy. At this time, the Tsarist government began to apply pressure on the Doukhobors to accept military service, imprisoning and brutally flogging those who continued to resist. They were exiled to Georgia—men, women and children—under conditions that suggested the whole community would slowly die of sickness and starvation.

Two great Russians with international reputations intervened. Piotr Kropotkin had travelled across Canada and had been impressed by the success with which groups of Mennonites, also from Russia, had been settled on the prairies. He immediately suggested to the Tolstoyans who were running a relief committee in London that the Canadian West might be the ideal place for the Doukhobors to take flight to, particularly as Clifford Sifton, the new minister of the interior, favoured the immigration of eastern European peasants to fill the great void of the prairies now that the CPR had been completed. Tolstoy offered the royalties of his last novel, *Resurrection*, to pay for the passage to Canada, and eventually about eight thousand Doukhobors arrived. Meanwhile, Kropotkin's friend, James Mavor, had helped negotiate the deal by which Doukhobors living in villages could receive individual quarter sections of land and cultivate them communally as a block. It was specified by the Doukhobors, and agreed by the immigration authorities in the presence of witnesses like Aylmer Maude, that taking an oath of allegiance to the Queen would not be required. It was to be, like the Indian treaties, an agreement easily broken.

On the whole, the Doukhobors were given good lands, and other settlers envied them, but they remained secure until Sifton was replaced as minister by Frank Oliver, who favoured the idea of individual over collective landholding and saw advantages in giving the land to pioneer farmers who would eventually vote, rather than to Doukhobors who kept out of politics. The homestead regulations were now applied in all their rigour, and the lands of those who refused to swear allegiance were taken and distributed among the crowds of applicants that surrounded the prairie land offices when the confiscation took place. A majority of the Douk-hobors—more than six thousand led by Peter the Lordly—crossed the mountains to form the Christian Community of Universal Brotherhood on land bought in British Columbia. There they were persecuted by the provincial authorities over matters like education (they refused to send their children to schools where they feared militarism might be inculcated) and registration of births and deaths, matters they felt rested between them and God. The Doukhobors developed their own striking campaigns of resistance, which included nude parades and arson. Hundreds of them were imprisoned, and at one time a special concentration camp was established for them on Peers Island. The most scandalous example of governmental arbitrariness occurred when the RCMP swept through the Doukhobor villages in the Kootenays, arresting all the children they could find and taking them to a camp in New Denver where they were force-educated, an act remembered with anger by whole generations of Doukhobors.

Wiser counsels eventually prevailed on both sides, and by the late 1960s, the vigour had died out of the Doukhobor protests, while adaptable teachers had found means of making education more acceptable. Peripheral issues like registration had lost their interest. The Doukhobor lands—which during the 1930s were foreclosed by the Canada Trust and redeemed by the provincial government—were returned at a price to individual Doukhobors, and the communitarian urge of the sect has not revived. What the Doukhobors have retained is their pacifism, which the federal government sensibly refrained from testing in two world wars, and their special kind of council in the form of *sobranie*, the assembly of the faithful, where the psalms recording Doukhobor beliefs and the Doukhobor past are sung and the spiritual leader seeks and speaks the consensus of the gathering.

III

IN MY ESSAY ON THE NATIVE PEOPLES, I pointed toward a latent hostility between politically democratic societies and the consensual ones that offer their viable alternatives. It has occurred in Canada in the difficulties between provincial governments and, as well as the Doukhobors, the Hutterite communities which hold their land in common and are ruled—if that is an even remotely appropriate term—by their male elders. Hutterite society is not democracy as many of us conceive it, since the women have little to say in the general direction of the community, and children are raised under strict and spartan conditions. Yet in its proper roles in the material world, which are economic, social and above all agricultural, the Hutterite commune has proved successful in sustaining itself in a largely hostile environment, and through times of crisis when the outer society with its individualist ethics and economics has suffered much more severely.

Another case—a classic one we have already glimpsed—was the clash between an authoritarian nineteenth-century form of democracy masquerading as an individualist one and a genuine consensual society. This conflict was between the Métis and the Americanized Ontarian speculators who entered the plains of Rupert's Land as the Hudson's Bay Company's hegemony broke down at the end of the 1860s.

In our histories of this period, we have tended to emphasize the opposition between different systems of land measurement and ownership that undoubtedly existed and helped precipitate the Métis rebellions of 1870 and 1885. We have underplayed the specific democratic achievements made by the Métis during this period of change and brought to an end by external forces.

The Métis were in fact the first to recognize the need to reorganize their essentially nomadic existence to suit the new circumstances. They began with their marvellously efficient organization of the buffalo hunt, developed from that of the Cree, with individuals placed by general consent in places of limited and temporary authority. The idea of limited and temporary authority, inherited from the Indians, combined with an extreme love of freedom and distrust of set laws inherited from the community's French fathers, the *coureurs de bois* who were virtual self-exiles from the authority-ridden *ancien regime*. It was this European element, this idea of freedom as something to be desired and defined and protected, that led the Métis to go beyond the Indian bounds of custom and to create the commune of St. Laurent, with its mutually agreed hunt and land and forest regulations, and its simple criminal code of rustic punishments; sometimes beating, sometimes pillorying for a time with the crime written on a placard hung around the condemned man's neck (few Métis could read the message, for like Dumont himself, they were mostly illiterate but they knew what the paper or the bit of wood meant), sometimes confiscation of horses or destruction of equipment. Métis custom allowed for death as a punishment for especially atrocious crimes, but I have never seen a record of its having been put into practice. As for imprisonment, there was no gaol in St. Laurent, and the idea of shutting a man away from the sun and the wind and the back of a horse would have been repugnant in the extreme to the Métis with their strong sense of freedom.

Through the short life of the St. Laurent commune, the Métis proved—at a transition phase in the prairies—that their kind of consensual democracy could work as well in a settlement as in a nomadic hunting camp. If the Canadian authorities had been willing to learn from these prairie people and to use their example of wise self-government in developing the new territories of the West with the co-operation of the Native peoples already there, there might never have been a North-West Rebellion in 1885.

From such examples we can draw several lessons. The first

is that in a society fated by geography and history to be as diverse as Canada's, one proceeds through this diversity and uses it to create a tentative and ever adaptable unity. That means tolerating and even encouraging varieties of democratic organization that may be outside one's tastes or traditions. A vital and varied society is developed where people of many kinds and outlooks fulfill their lives in their own ways.

The second lesson is that the real shape of a society, the basic form through which it can grow to a fruitful maturity, is found at the local level, where simplicity of structure can combine with a special sensitivity to the geography and history of the locality, to the human and natural environments as they mingle. This has been the kind of situation toward which some of the most promising social trends of recent times have moved, without total failure, without ultimate success.

IV

THERE WAS, FOR EXAMPLE, the movement of local collectivization, inspired by the anarchists of Spain after the civil war began in 1936. In Andalusia, Valencia, Catalonia and a great deal of Aragon, the villagers took over the lands in their localities, expropriating the estates of absentee landlords and inspiring small-scale peasants to pool their fields. In the cities, factories and utilities were taken over and operated by their workers, sometimes with the help of former managers or even owners making the best of a situation.

The takeovers astonished everyone who had talked beforehand about anarchist impracticality. Crops increased in the villages, and for the first time everyone was fed. The factories kept on producing and increased their output to meet the needs of the civil war. The Spanish communes, which non-anarchist observers like Franz Borkenau visited with great interest and wrote about with admiration, appear to have been perfectly viable in their proper spheres, the social and the economic. It was the intrusion of hostile politics that destroyed them, when the communist columns, led into Aragon by General Lister, began to destroy the communes, jealous of their success, even before Franco and his foreign legionaries had a chance.

It was also politics that at least delayed Gandhi's great vision of a free India, that would be based on a revival of rural economy and would unite in various confederal ways layers of peoples speaking many languages and holding many beliefs. The ecumenicism of his quasi-religious gatherings, with their hymns from all creeds, was reflected in his vision for the arrangement of the land.

Gandhi was never in any narrow way an Indian nationalist. He did not want merely to set India free from the British so that it might fall under the rule of native power brokers. He wanted to liberate the country from all outdated systems of power and privilege, from the oppression of native landowners and moneylenders as much as the Raj's tax collectors, from obedience to the caste system as well as to the laws of the British. And he understood that this could only be done successfully by organizing the villages into a decentralized confederation of local confederations, and educating them into communes of equals, their small societies supported by largely self-sufficient economies in which organic farming, small workshops and handcraft industries would provide both work and assured income. In this way, an end might be brought to ancient native corruption, and at the same time an ancient, complex but decayed economy might be revived and made the centre of a free society.

Gandhian organization failed to establish itself in India in 1947, despite Gandhi's immense personal prestige, for his proposal that India should avoid the perils of state power came at a time when the idea of the nation-state was undergoing a great revival, partly because European nations once occupied by the Axis powers were busy re-creating themselves, and partly because, in the rapid débâcle of the empires that followed the liberation of India through the 1950s and into the 1970s, so many of the former colonies were eager to reproduce on a large or small scale the very realms to which they had been subject. Jawaharlal Nehru, whose education included years at the English public school Harrow, and Cambridge University, immediately set up a state that imitated the Raj and continued to do so in some extraordinary ways; for example, though Britain and most other civilized countries have given up the death penalty, they still hang in India, the country of Buddha and Gandhi. And when Indira Gandhi decided to declare an emergency, she reached back into the Raj's archives and invoked a viceregal decree from the 1930s.

India, so promising a soil for a fresh concept of social arrangement to take form, did become a federation, but mainly because its many languages each demanded a homeland. But within the federal pattern, state and federation share out power in a way that gives little room for free organization through the village panchayats; for real economic and social decentralism one has to turn to some of the smaller former colonies, like Samoa and Fiji, where the old pre-colony landholding lineages have re-emerged as the essential local units.

Rejected by the Congress leaders, when they tasted the blood of power, Gandhi's ideas were left to his devoted followers. Vinoba Bhave expressed them most sensationally in his peregrinations across India, begging land for the poor,

which other Gandhians are now turning into fruitful farms
for harijans; there are other groups working on the far edge of
poverty, trying to help tribal peoples whose life has been
disrupted by the death of the jungles, and often succeeding
by developing local energies among the poorest of people that
were not revealed until help was offered. (Having worked with
such Gandhians, raising money in Canada for them, I know
the potentialities of local organization among people often so
facilely dismissed as primitive. Give them hope and only a
little material help, and they can do, as Gandhi knew,
amazing things.)

V

TODAY, AT THE END OF THE TWENTIETH CENTURY, we
live in a different world from that of 1947. The old-fashioned
nation-state is following the obsolete empires into extinction, at the same time as the people—individuals or collec-
tivities—are demanding more direct involvement in the
administration of affairs and situations that determine the
courses of their lives. Perhaps we do not talk so much as we
did about the elimination of power, but we are talking, in
Vaclav Havel's phrase, of "the power of the powerless," and
the disempowerment of the powerful, whether individual or
corporate. The complexity of political structures and the
sheer magnitude of collective endeavours in a world of
financial and industrial rather than political imperialism,
has led some of the most enlightened of contemporary social
thinkers, like Lewis Mumford and Noam Chomsky and Paul
Goodman, to look at the roots of power, to realize that it is
controllable and must be controlled on the level at which
men and women can participate directly in decisions affect-

ing their lives. Government, administration, whatever one may call it, must abandon the assumption that there is a ruling class that "knows best" how the rest of society must live. All authority must henceforward be derived from the principle that those most directly involved in a situation extending beyond the competence of the free individual must deal with it on the simplest and most local level.

A special urgency has been given to the need for local decision making by the increasing importance of environmental considerations in the lives of human communities. Essentially, every situation of environment at peril becomes evident first of all on a local level, even if its sources are outside the locality. Sometimes it can be dealt with among neighbours or on a hamlet level. A creek or lake problem may require that several such groups come together to safeguard the purity of the waters and the agricultural or sylvan productivity of its shores. A village or county assembly may be needed to bring all interest groups together and perhaps repel the intrusion of outside industrial interests.

There were examples of this kind of co-operation in many parts of the world before peoples turned to the political path and found a fatal solution in the nation-state. The ancient Teutons, including Angles and Saxons, had their folkmoots, gatherings of the people to vote on matters of general interest; they antedated the kings. The Swiss *Landesgemeinden*, the small and ancient mountain cantons, where all the citizens meet on one day a year to vote their laws and both the voters and the administrating councillors they elect swear solemn oaths to maintain what is voted on that day, provide a toughly surviving variant of the folkmoot of ancient times, and so, at a further remove, did the town meetings instituted by the English dissenters when they arrived on the free soil of New England. Another tradition, that of the Greek city republics with their variants of direct democracy, was preserved in the Italian medieval city republics, of which San Marino is today the last survivor.

Apart from the Native peoples, including the Métis, Canada has little in the way of communal tradition of this kind, since it was settled largely by government-controlled immigration supervised and circumscribed by the North-West Mounted Police. But all over western Canada since the 1960s, the sense of communalism, the desire for the devolution of authority and the empowerment of local groups to deal with local concerns, has grown steadily. At the same time, the sense that the present federal-provincial division of powers fails local interests has grown on a wide scale.

It is there not merely in villages that cannot protect themselves against intrusive logging or polluting industry because the requisite powers are retained by higher levels of authority. It exists also in the metropolitan cities, whose local life is rich, varied and strong, and which are not only centres of national culture but also great cosmopolitan centres through which the wisdom of the world penetrates our existence. The divorce between political formalities and the general cultural development of the country is particularly evident in provinces like Québec and British Columbia, where the emergence of both Montréal and Vancouver as cosmopolitan centres has been impeded by the domination of small and narrow-visioned local capitals like Québec City and Victoria. Every local authority in Canada is indeed liable to the veto of a provincial or federal authority for the simple reason that the level of municipal competence, the true basic level of democratic decision making, has been effectively frustrated in any constitutional Canadian document up to now by the absence of provisions for independent municipal action. Nor has there been any attempt to define the areas of local governmental competence as there was under the BNA for the federal and the provincial governments. Local governments, which should be the basis of any viable polity, exist now on the sufferance of provincial authorities, which grant them narrow charters and deliberately reduce their scope of action.

In the changed, multilevel and multifunctional shape that I envisage for a future Canada, the local bodies, town or village councils elected annually and as far as possible directly, would be linked politically with the provincial governments, under charters extending their present independence of action in parochial affairs to the limits of the Bill of Rights, for here authority is nearest home. But in matters economic and social, and especially environmental, it would be linked with the regional councils, through which in any case all environmental questions extending beyond the municipal local group should be administered, with initiatives, generally speaking, coming from the localities. It is possible, of course, that within the localities there may be deep differences of opinion or interest, and provision should be made for granting to neighbourhood or other special interest groups the opportunity of being heard whenever a decision is made relating to their immediate locality. The custom of neighbourhood meetings relating to innovations or eliminations should be made universal, so that people should not erect hideous buildings that interfere with views or ancient lights, or cut down beautiful trees that the neighbourhood has long cherished.

Libertarian though I have always been, and in some ways to extremity, it has always been with a Proudhonian sense that, in terms of property, we are not at liberty to treat wilfully the products of civilization we have inherited from the labour and intelligence of our ancestors; we should not disdain and destroy the heritage of an environment the geological eras have bequeathed to us. We must regard all property as a trust, to be administered for the well-being of humankind and other living beings. This is already recognized in many directions; nobody really objects to sound regulations for the treatment of sewage or for discouraging fires that pollute the atmosphere. Yet the idea of managing the aesthetic aspects of the environment, as distinct from its hygienic ones, has not been accepted in most Canadian cities, though it has in many European ones. There have been repeated recent cases, in Vancouver and doubtless in other cities, of speculators moving in and felling on the properties they have bought trees that brought pride and pleasure to the whole neighbourhood, without the neighbours or the city council being able to stop them.

It seems, as the sentiment of the public in most countries now suggests, that we have reached the stage in governmental evolution when the voice of the individual should be given a hearing, and especially on the local matters that concern him most directly in his daily life. If any change is proposed on a private property that might affect the appearance or character of a neighbourhood, the town or village council should take it under consideration, make sure that the households of the locality are informed, and then call a neighbourhood meeting where the issues would be argued until consensus prevails. (The likelihood these days is that the consensus will move toward the preservation of the neighbourhood as it now exists.)

From backstreet disputes about felling trees and region-wide environmental decisions, to the transformation of parliamentary systems and the metamorphosis of the irremediably corrupt old Senate into a vital Chamber of Regions, this book has been moving on a wide area of public concerns and reaching down into the heart of society, because the interconnections of a vital polity are necessarily complex, and neglect of the relations between human beings and families and neighbourhoods can announce the disease of whole societies. As Blake put it in that extraordinary series of revolutionary maxims, "Auguries of Innocence":

> A dog starved at his master's gate
> predicts the ruin of the State.

There is no reality too remote, no group too small to have its rights, whose despising or disregarding can set going a landslide of the whole political structure. This is how revolutions often begin. So let us care first for the small affairs of society, the modest group, the formerly powerless individual, the misfit, the madman whom wiser societies have revered. The larger problems will not go away if we do this, but we shall face them with a new understanding and a new strength.

By giving meaning in this way to the smallest groups in our society, to our most local interests and endeavours, we shall be creating a genuinely pluralist order out of which initiatives hard to imagine in our present society will emerge. When the unimaginative federal and provincial hierarchies that control such areas as the protection of the environment and the proper use of its resources have been dissolved, when the local people to whom stewardship in these matters naturally belongs are allowed to act according to their local knowledge and experienced judgement, we may be nearer to solving the essential problems of our world than we have been at any time since the industrial revolution began its destructive work. What I suggest in my proposals is not a way of breaking up society; it is, on the contrary, a way of making its links more durable and interpenetrative. What I propose is not a thousand isolationist communities within a region, but an infinity of clusters of local groups which can deal with problems they share on various levels, whether it is guarding an estuary from pollution, or creating a kind of free rural university, or turning an exhausted peat digging into a combination sewage treatment plant and truck farm, or protecting and sustaining an imperilled wildlife habitat. When we have learned to co-operate extensively in such matters, we may be better equipped to deal with the second-ary political issues.

The intent is always achieving the special unity that comes from diversity; the two conditions are dependent on each other, for true unity is not a synonym for homogeneity. It can be seen better in terms of complementarity, the kind of fruitful balance that emerges from the fortunate mingling of many forms of life into an ecosystem.

It is an extendable kind of unity, in nature the condition of a tiny marsh but also of a vast prairie or a great forest, and in a country the same processes operate as in a county. The bonds that actually operate on a countrywide—or in Canada's case on a continent-wide scale—are in fact bonds of culture and communication, which are the subject of my next essay. They are the bonds that may help a fervent British Colum-bian or Québecois say in the end, "I am Canadian too." But they are the most fragile of bonds, and in recent years have been disastrously neglected.

6

ROADS OF IRON,
WAVES OF POWER

I

THE CLASSIC EMPIRES have always depended on their great systems of transport and communication, and so have the continent-wide nations. Centuries before the Romans, the Persians laid down their network of highways that linked Persepolis with Smyrna and Thebes in one direction, and with India in the other. The Incas united their Andean empire, from Ecuador south to Bolivia, with solid stone roads, some of which are still in use today. The Portuguese and the Dutch and, above all, the British united their small heartlands with vast Asian and African trading grounds by the highways of the sea, which they protected with their navies and with colonies along the way that acted as maritime depots and later as coaling stations. And in nineteenth- and early twentieth-century North America, more than anywhere else in the world, financiers and politicians used the railway for multiple purposes—to unite a continent between sea and sea, to open the uninhabited regions to settlement, and to provide the means for making gestures of military warning.

The history of the American frontier, as I have remarked elsewhere, is somewhat different from that of the Canadian West, and must be considered separately, since many of the factors that operated south of the Forty-ninth Parallel did not apply in Canada. So far as Canada is concerned, the essential point in the context of this book is that the building of a railway gave substance to the vision of a country extending from "ocean even unto ocean," once the aim of those we so significantly call the Fathers of *Confederation*. The provision of a railway was not indeed covered by a clause in the BNA. But its need soon became evident if confederation were to be implemented, and since it figures in the agreement by which British Columbia entered, which was a kind of supplementary document to the constitutional act itself, it must be regarded as covered by Canada's founding compacts. The hesitations of the federal government in actually beginning the railway almost wrecked the confederal plan when British Columbia threatened to secede, and the audacity with which it was finally built over vast plains and chains of mountains to bring a colony of about thirty thousand people into Canada was perhaps the greatest of all manifestations of confederal zeal.

The Canadian Pacific Railway (CPR) was to be succeeded by other ventures aimed at uniting the nation in terms of transport and communications, through airlines, roads and the various electronic media, where the variety of initiatives and responsibilities established a uniquely Canadian pattern of state action mingling with private enterprise, and federal mingling with provincial initiative.

Demographic problems led the various governments before and after Confederation into becoming involved in the kind of transportation and communication ventures that were generally regarded as the province of private, profit-gathering ownership south of the border. Even today, Canada is a relatively thinly populated land, and in the decades after 1812, when its economic and political structures were taking shape, it was far less populous than the countries of Europe or even the United States. The natural waterways had to be supplemented for defensive as well as commercial purposes by canals that avoided difficult stretches of navigation, but there was as yet neither a large number of people to use them nor the capital to build them and sustain them through the pioneer years. Both the Lachine and Welland canals were started by private entrepreneurs, but eventually taken over by the colonial government of Upper Canada. The Rideau Canal was considered necessary to provide a militarily feasible link between the St. Lawrence and Ottawa rivers that would be out of danger of immediate American attack, and for this reason it was built and operated by the British military authorities.

Thus, by the time the railways were being built, a special Canadian pattern for transport undertakings had been established, a pattern of caution and compromise. Private syndicates proposed and began work on the railways, but politicians quickly became involved in both the speculative and the legislative side of the process. Sir Allan McNab, leader of the Tory opposition in the province of Canada in 1853, who doubled as president of the Great Western Railway, spoke for many of his kind when he said, "Railroads are my politics." It was a statement of reality rather than a jest.

Railways served the community and the individuals who were their passengers and who had found travel hard and arduous before the trains began to run. But, apart from their profits from transporting goods and people, the railways profited through the generosity of a community convinced of the need for them. Large grants of land were given by both federal and provincial governments for the tracks and depots, but also for speculative sale. Government-guaranteed loans were an early means of collecting capital, which was drawn largely from Britain and the United States. Eventually, to push a scheme over the top toward completion, direct cash grants might be made.

So emerged a network of privately owned railways which involved the public purse in their massive indebtedness, and which at the same time had managed to accumulate massive land and mineral rights. In the West, through the prairies, across the Rockies and down to the Pacific, a whole cluster of railroads were built to service the areas not reached by the CPR, which concentrated on the mineral-rich south along the border. The Grand Trunk Pacific reached salt water at Prince Rupert; the Canadian Northern reached Vancouver by a different route from the CPR. And the Pacific Great Eastern (PGE), a line meant to link the Cariboo and the country north of Prince George with Burrard Inlet, was only completed, despite generous land grants and loan guarantees, between two hardly known places, Quesnel and Squamish. By the end of World War One, all these railways were bankrupt, yet they were needed to populate and sustain industry in the areas they served. There was no alternative but for governments to intervene directly. Ottawa acquired by foreclosure the Grand Trunk, the Grand Trunk Pacific, the Canadian Northern and a number of lesser links in eastern Canada, and incorporated them into the nationally owned Canadian National (CN). At the same time, the government of British Columbia acquired the PGE, which continued its rustic primitive progress through the ranchlands and mountains between Quesnel and Squamish, a tiny port on Howe Sound. After the accession of Social Credit to power in the late 1950s, the PGE was extended south of its originally proposed terminus at North Vancouver on Burrard Inlet, and northward to the Yukon border.

Thus, the Canadian railways became partly privately and partly publicly owned, and the same applied when air transport developed, and the industry was divided between the publicly owned Air Canada and a number of private airlines that eventually came together as Canadian Airlines International. The regulation of transport and communications under the BNA was a matter of dispute between the Ottawa government and the provinces, but it was finally decided by the courts to be a federal field. This did not mean, however, that state *operation* became universal; with the advent of radio and later television, a familiar pattern emerged of a publicly owned system, the Canadian Broadcasting Corporation (CBC), and licensed privately owned stations and networks that competed with the public network.

The regulation of transportation and communication, according to the BNA, are obligations laid principally on the federal government; so, presumably, is the provision and maintenance of adequate services in these areas, if the treaty between British Columbia and Canada in 1870 is to be taken seriously. National ownership, no matter whether it is sustained by government departments or Crown corporations, implies ownership by the people, and in some way or another the constitution should ensure in these vital areas of unification the convenience of the people, in terms of transport, and the needs of a pluralist and regionalist society in terms of communication.

Recent governments have not provided that ensurance. The cutdown in railway passenger services may be within the letter of the law, in the sense that a minimal service between Vancouver and the Toronto–Montréal axis is maintained, but it is not in accordance with the spirit of the original treaty, since an adequate passenger service throughout Canada is certainly not sustained; while the possible use of the railway as a potent educational instrument, by filling all the vacant coaches with school children learning at first hand about Canada, never enters the unimaginative heads of the politicians who talk of uniting Canada but never recognize the means by which this might be done.

II

SIMILARLY, IN THE FIELD OF COMMUNICATION, successive governments, no matter whether Liberal or Conservative, have failed to insist that the CBC, as a national broadcasting service, should interpret positively its dual mandate, to promote understanding among the peoples of the various regions of Canada, and to sustain the arts, which are the essential manifestation of the Canadian cultures.

It is obvious that such matters lie outside politics, and that in cultural fields the interference of politicians, with their attempts to use the arts for their own purposes, has been positively deleterious. Hardly less negative has been the preoccupation with metropolitan concerns that comes inevitably when a centralized power structure, whether a government or a large private corporation, is in charge of transport or communications. It was not without cause that the people of the prairies so long maintained their hostility to the great national railways controlled from Montréal. And the main fault of the CBC has been the centralization that makes it deaf to local needs.

Quite evidently, we face a contradiction between a concept of central control and one of co-ordination among regions and localities; the first is linked to the idea of authority and the second to that of consensus. Centralization assumes that, however large and varied the area involved, the appropriate nationwide authority can make decisions that will work, a view that led Communist leaders in Russia and China to perilous extremes. To succeed, it demands a fairness of intent that is rare in politics, and a detailed awareness of regional needs that is almost impossible to acquire in actuality. But politicians have faith in "easy" homogenous processes, and that is why we have had in Canada such anomalous situations as those in which a federal government obsessed with the phantom of "nationality" (as Canadian ones usually are) busily went about, virtually destroying the passenger facilities of VIA Rail that in Canadian minds symbolized the idea of a country continuing and connected from ocean unto ocean. We may have felt no particular desire to support the CPR as a commercial and politically manipulative entity, for it was notably antisocial in its activities where profit gathering was involved, but the fact remains that it and its successor helped to create among us the concept of a Canada whose national identity was more than the sum of its parts; this the CBC also tried to do in its pristine decentralist days when organization by region—regions listening to each other—was regarded as essential to its operations.

We are back, I suggest, in the area of choosing whether

our priorities are political or socioeconomic, and this means a return to considering the conflict between the nation-state and the confederation of regions that lies at the heart of our present Canadian dilemma. Matters of transport and communication may well be political in their inception. To fill out hastily the pattern of a transcontinental British North America, the relatively young dominion agreed in 1870 to build the railway between Ontario and the Pacific that became the CPR, and in 1876 to assume the debts of Prince Edward Island's new railway, so as to bring these colonies into confederation. These, initially, were political moves; not for almost two decades would the CPR show its social and economic importance as, with increasing speed, it populated and created a whole new society in the prairies. The railways and the later developed means of transport and communication (including that special Canadian innovation, the telephone) showed their importance by implementing in material and human terms the confederation of Canada. They respond to basic local and human needs, and to remove all such services from the political level, where they will always tend toward deadening centralization, seemed to me one of the essential tasks involved in the recreation of Canada, on which we should now be engaged.

III

ONE OF THE QUESTIONS THAT OFTEN ARISES is how transport and communications over as vast an area as Canada's may conceivably be carried out without some centralized authority. Here I suggest we might consider a well-functioning international model. When he wrote his classic work, *Mutual Aid*, almost a hundred years ago, the anarchist Piotr

Kropotkin stressed that many of the functions necessary for the proper running of society operated on a voluntary basis, with no question of state planning or overriding authorities. He found this to be particularly the case with transport and communication-related functions, such as railways and postal services; an International Postal Union was founded in 1878, to co-ordinate the transmission of mail between various countries and continents, and within ten years it had fifty-five members, then including all the important independent countries. In the same spirit, an International Railway Congress was established to deal with matters like transshipment of goods and passengers, and with facilitating the development of the great international trains of the nineteenth century, like the Orient Express, into today's Eurorail system. Such organizations have never in any way been overriding authorities even to the limited degree of the United Nations or the European community. They do their work at gatherings where delegations speak for the various national organizations, and decisions are reached by general consensus or by closed discussions between the groups most involved in specific issues. The reputation for efficiency among such international organizations is high and has been sustained in spite of the interruptions due to international conflicts.

There is no reason why, if we give a regional structure to our country on an economic and social level, as I have suggested, transport and communications systems should not be controlled just as efficiently as now (or more so, if one thinks of Canada Post) by representatives of the regions and the various social groups. Unfortunately, in their beginnings, Canadian communications systems were created to further the political motives of Sir John A. Macdonald's

Conservative party and to bring profits to the entrepreneurs who organized the railway projects—and, in many cases, unloaded their failing companies onto the taxpayer. Having lured British Columbia into confederation by promising a railway, the central government showed no inclination to build it until the calls for secession in British Columbia grew too loud to disregard, while the importance of such a link with Macdonald's ambitiously centralizing National Plan became evident.

Neither the railway system nor the post office in Canada has ever been seriously directed toward the interests of the people or the interests of the localities, and this applies also to later developments like plane travel and broadcasting. In fact, the peculiar Canadian combination of state and private ownership has worked negatively in this respect, so that even services clearly meant originally to serve the interests of the people, like the post office, are forced to show a profit; this they do by cutting necessary services and loosening the network of contact and relationships that the communications systems were intended to foster in creating a natural, as distinct from an artificial and political, Canadian unity.

IV

BUT IF, LIKE SO MANY OTHER COUNTRIES, Canada has a history of communications systems managed (or rather mismanaged) through their domination by centralized political and commercial interests, there are alternative examples. Already I have talked in political terms of the advantage of countries oriented toward the communal and the local; here, in terms of transport, one reaches a similar conclusion. If we were to reorganize our public transport systems for the benefit of the public, we should not look to the larger countries, communist or capitalist, for examples. My own adventures on the Chinese railways taught me to take seriously the laments of those who had responded to the romantic call of following the Russian trans-Siberian railway to its end; trains were run for the convenience of People's Liberation Army generals and party cadres. In India, where the railway system has hardly changed since it was the pride of the Raj sixty years ago, I was able to recognize how relatively useless to the Indian people (billions of them living in still largely inaccessible villages) was a railway system designed for imperial defence. And I am only one of the millions of people appalled by the way in which both Canadian and American governments as well as railway companies have abandoned the service of localities, individual passengers and small entrepreneurs to concentrate on the profits of the long, heavy haul.

When I did find a railway system that had been both well sustained and used for the benefit of communities and their inhabitants, it was (once again!) in Switzerland, the most decentralized as well as one of the smallest and most densely populated countries of Europe. In his recent book, *Freedom to Go: After the Motor Age*, the British writer Colin Ward recollected an essay which he and I had read with great interest in an issue of *Encounter* thirty years before. It was by the Swiss man of letters (well known in his own country), Herbert Leuthy, and it was called "Has Switzerland a Future." Leuthy believed that Switzerland had a future precisely in the directions of centralist organization neglected by its European neighbours,

and the simplest example was the Swiss railway system, which is the densest network in the world. At great cost and with great trouble, it has been made to serve the needs of smallest localities and most remote valleys, not as a paying proposition but because such was the will of the people. It is the outcome of fierce political struggles. In the nineteenth century the "democratic railway movement" brought the small Swiss communities into conflict with the big towns, which had plans for centralization . . . .

And if we compare the Swiss system with the French which, with admirable geographical regularity, is entirely centred on Paris so that the prosperity or the decline, the life or death, of whole systems has depended on the quality of the link with the capital, we see the difference between a centralized state and a federal alliance. The railway map is the easiest to read at a glance, but let us now superimpose on it another showing economic activity and the movement of population. The distribution of industrial activity all over Switzerland, even in the outlying areas, accounts for the strength and stability of the social structure of the country and prevented those horrible nineteenth-century concentrations of industry, with their slums and rootless proletariat.

As anyone who has spent even a short time in industrialized northern Switzerland—where the fields are dotted with small nonpolluting factories and workshops fed by abundant supplies of electricity—will have realized, the Swiss have managed much more felicitously than most Europeans or North Americans to balance industrial and rural life. Swiss people often work in cities, like Zurich or Basel or Luzern, and continue to live on small holdings in their original communes. There are few real satellite communities or

156

suburbs in Switzerland, where the local communes existed and developed their characters before the cities spread out to unite with them in what is still a meeting of political equals. Commuting goes on, but the outer communes, the city's hinterland, do not become mere bedroom settlements, scattered over the landscape where it suits developers.

This special relationship between town and country has been made sustainable not only by the railways that maintain their services even in unprofitable situations, but also by the virtually ubiquitous Post Auto services that open the remotest places to the rural wanderer. There is no valley too scantily populated, no complex of country roads too straggling to have its bus service, carrying mail and picking up passengers, and often running more than once a day. The losses on the Post Autos are made up by the profits of the telephone system, which the post office controls and which in its turn profits from Switzerland's international role as financial broker. Thus, the gnomes of Zurich, about whom we used to hear so much, pay for one of the world's best country bus services, looping along Switzerland's intricate lakeshores and into its scantily populated mountain valleys.

The difference from Canada, where we have seen—in federal and provincial hands—a steady diminution in the scope and quality of local transport services, must be obvious. It is not merely that historic arrangements, hallowed by treaties between the original colonies and the confederation, are treated here with contempt. It is even more that managerial convenience and profit have overruled popular wishes and popular convenience, and that this has happened as much through the state capitalist bodies known as Crown corporations as through the privately owned combines. Apart from the cuts in rail services, Canada Post—

which never had a rural equivalent of the Swiss Post Auto—
has deliberately disrupted the network of rural communities
by depriving the smaller and more remote ones of the
crossroad store post offices that have made Canada's regional
societies so close a network of roots.

V

THE ROOTS OF REGIONAL SOLIDARITY AND IDENTITY
indeed rest in ease and quickness of communication, and
increasingly we have come to the dangerous and contrary
situation where physical exchanges have been largely replaced by electronic ones. The electronic media, starting
with the telegraph and the telephone, have meant that over
the past century, communities and individuals have been in
more instant and immediate communication than ever
before. The importance of the telegraph as a means of
communication tended to diminish with the decline of the
railroad, but the invention of fax has added a visual dimen-
sion to the telephone. These are all matters of easier communication, and are obviously to be welcomed, as are the
broader manifestations of communication that come together under the general heading of broadcasting: radio and
television. Here, however, we encounter a factor that brings
all means of transport and communications into the legitimate field of the constitution maker, whose problem is
salting the tail of diversity in a society drifting toward the
swamp of homogeneity, which is the expected result of an
unremitting and obsessive search for "unity." We have to
protect our natural links and to root out the centralizers
where they have become established, which in Canada

means a transformation of the organizations regulating and carrying out broadcasting.

A few futurists and utopian writers may have conceived the possibility of wireless communication by the time the BNA was passed into law in 1867, but it was not one of the fields specifically assigned to either the federal or the provincial governments. It became a subject of dispute between Ottawa and the provinces during the 1920s, and eventually reached the Judicial Committee of the Privy Council which, surprisingly, considering its generally pro-provincial inclinations, ruled in favour of the federal government. As a result, general control of broadcasting remained with the central government, though the fact that education was one of the fields controlled by the provinces meant that in this area they were allowed to establish their own local services; some of these, such as TV Ontario, did originate a fair amount of high-quality local output.

Nationally controlled by bodies like the Board of Broadcast Governors and, more recently, the Canadian Radio and Television Commission (CRTC), the broadcasting services in Canada have been divided between the privately owned networks and the public ones, the CBC and a few provincial education-oriented enterprises. The private groups have never been other than imitators of American commercial broadcasting with all its vulgarizing and homogenizing tendencies. Their main function has been low-level entertainment that makes a profit. The efforts of bodies like the CRTC to impose "Canadian content" have been useless because even where the performers and their music are Canadian by origin, their style and the culture they project are continental North American.

With the CBC, two other factors entered in and played

their part in broadcasting politics up to the later 1960s. The CBC was first regarded as a means by which the regions could find expression and speak to each other in ways that could lead to cultural unity within Canada. With this in mind, the regional organization of the CBC was at first strong and well financed, and when I returned to Canada in 1949, I found active centres of regional broadcasting that competed as well as co-operating with the central network.

I also found it was the only organization that in those days would employ me as a writer. In its earlier years and even decades, CBC programs played a very important role in the postwar development of Canadian arts, acting as a patron–employer where none else existed. In literature, for example, it helped develop a tradition during the 1940s and 1950s; in terms of popular practical criticism, Robert Weaver—who produced programs like "Critically Speaking" and "Anthology"—was much more important than, say, Northrop Frye.

The CBC encouraged poets, older and younger, to read their works over the air. And it virtually kept the short story alive as a form at times when neither book publishers nor magazine editors were inclined to publish brief fiction.

In drama, CBC performed two important functions. Radio offered a field for writers to develop theatrical writing at a time when the theatre in Canada had almost gone out of existence. And it gave employment to actors and producers, so that the dramatic arts did not die out, and when a revival of live theatre took place during the 1960s, people were there on all levels to give it life. A local musical tradition was also kept alive by the organization of symphony orchestras—some of the best of which were regional—and by commissioning works by Canadian composers.

With the advent of television, much that had gone on in

160

radio was continued (though attempts to create a new tradition of Canadian television drama were mostly unsuccessful), and attention was drawn to visual artists by taking the public eye into their studios.

Throughout this period from the 1930s to the 1960s, the CBC performed three important functions. It accepted that development in the various arts—and particularly the literary, the dramatic and the musical—was necessary for the growth of a meaningful national culture, and it set out to use modern means of communication for this purpose. It recognized the strongly regional character of Canadian cultures and reflected that character in its operations. And it acted as a kind of patron of the arts by employing actors, musicians and writers, many of whom remained in Canada because of the basic income it provided.

It is hard to determine why the original and highly productive policy of fostering the arts in a setting of regional autonomy was abandoned, but there is no doubt that the CBC was manipulated politically by various governments from the late 1960s, obsessed as they were with the shifting ignis fatuus of "national unity" seen as something other than a harmony of regions. Pierre Elliott Trudeau's Jacobinical centralism might fade away, but it was to be replaced by a different and more traditionally imperialist variety of the nation-state cult sustained by the resurgent Tories. The CBC became dominated by political concerns; it was clearly against the interests of successive federal governments, or even of the opposition parties—NDP and Liberals—who both had their centralist ambitions, to return the CBC to the even partially regionalist structure of the early 1960s. At the same time, literature and the arts assumed a declining importance in CBC programming, and the fine literary and dramatic programs, which Americans just over the border used to listen to and envy, fell away; only a few vestigial programs like "Ideas" remain. The employment of writers, musicians and actors has declined so that it is less than a pretence even of patronage. If one regards a nation's culture as its life blood and the arts as the heart that circulates this fluid, then the CBC has lost its functions as originally conceived, except as a means of transmitting information somewhat less efficiently than the privately owned television and radio systems.

VI

HOW CAN THIS SITUATION BE CHANGED? First of all, surely, by a return to the regional realities of Canada, and—perhaps even more important—a recognition that this is potentially one of the most fruitful fields for experiment in creative, unpolitical control. There exists—if it survives— a League for Public Broadcasting, which proceeds from the undeniable fact that the CBC is being threatened by partisan politicians who feel it should be an even more willing tool for their interests. But the public broadcasting advocates are led mainly by doctrinaire considerations; many are veteran social democrats who see the possibilities of the CBC as a bridgehead for their ideas, and fear—quite realistically—that its departure will open the way for a "broadcasting industry" dominated by commercial entrepreneurs. Their apprehensions may be justified; what is not justified is their support of the decayed and unreformed CBC of the 1990s, which bears no true relationship to the corporation in its active and productive years during the 1950s and the 1960s, and offers no effective shield against the spread of commercial values in broadcasting.

It is impossible to justify the expenditure of public money on the CBC as it exists, primarily because the only way in which it differs from the commercial networks is in being a convenient propaganda instrument for the government currently in power, a function the corporation accepts with grovelling willingness. "Public broadcasting" is not a phrase that conveys very much if one does not define "public." It can mean directly state-controlled broadcasting, or broadcasting by a public corporation like the present CBC in which the bureaucracy has become all-dominant, or some form of co-operative venture in which the really creative people control operations and the citizen-listeners have their advisory say in what they receive.

A new CBC, fostering harmony rather than homogeneity and respecting the regionally diverse nature of Canadian society, would leave such matters as entertainment, sports and so forth to the commercial networks, which in any case present them more effectively. It would concentrate on sustaining dialogue among regions by encouraging local self-expression; on once again presenting the arts lavishly as the truest manifestation of the Canadian spirit; on providing responsible news and public affairs programs. It would leave "popular culture" to the commercial networks—where, by definition, it belongs—and would not be scared of seeming elitist or being considered an overly academic institution, for it is among the universities, as an instrument for extending education and expanding awareness of our world, that in great part it belongs.

The heart and body of such a system would be the creators in their regions, supported by their citizen's advisory committees. There should be as little centralization as possible, although it is likely that certain programs should be national, broadcast in turn from the larger centres with more facilities, from Halifax to Vancouver and not excluding Yellowknife. The headquarters should be a co-ordinating agency well removed, for symbolic reasons, from Ottawa. A slight increase in the population of Seven Persons, Alberta, might be indicated. The main consideration should be the liberation of creativity from the dead weight of bureaucracy. Our collective imagination should never again be controlled by glib men and women at desks.

Here we are verging on "Ways and Means," the subject of the last essay, on how the changes I am proposing could be achieved and protected. Before that, there remains a further matter to be discussed. We are presumably agreed that the debate over the constitution is one that will continue, no matter what the politicians may do to close it off, until the people gain sufficient control over their lives and relationships. But what will be our relationships, as a confederation of people of many origins, with a world within which many of us have deep ancestral and cultural links?

7

CANADA IN THE ECOLOGY OF GLOBAL SOCIETY

I

IN NATURAL ECOLOGY, SECRETIVE HABITATS—a marsh, a pond—with populations of small animals, or vast settings of giant trees that give home to large animals, all play their parts in creating a distinctive natural system for a locality. And in the same way, in the global ecology of human societies that is revealed once one shakes free from the cloaking political abstractions, minor and even miniature localities and groups of localities are balanced by the larger relations of regions. Beyond that, there are clear resemblances between the relations of nations and the relations of, say, cities and villages within a nation. Unwittingly, doubtless unwillingly, the architects of the United Nations gave practical recognition to this fact when in the general assembly they accorded tiny states like Nauru and Tonga equal voices to the United States itself.

To determine the pattern of our relations with external communities—whether we talk of whole nations, or of neighbouring provinces each side of a border, or even of villages that share the same forest stretching into two countries—is as important for our political stability as arranging the relationship between local communities sharing the same watershed. It involves the application of political principles, and that is a constitutional matter, as external relations are in countries that aim at neutrality but realize they have international roles to play. Knowledge, communications, technologies, have condensed and homogenized our world, and even ancient Timbuctu and typical Dumbo in the Australian desert are no longer the Back of the Beyond. No person, and no community, can any longer survive in isolation, and to survive, as the poet said, we must love one another or die. Once, not many decades ago, there were indeed places in Canada, on the edges of the northern land mass and in the Arctic Archipelago, where mail arrived once a year, if the supply ship made it through the ice that season. But the remoteness of our "great lone land," as it used to be called, is as obsolete as those of the desert cities of Africa.

Human society in Canada has indeed been shaped by external factors from the time the first hunters crossed the Bering Land Bridge, perhaps fifteen millennia ago. The history of our peoples is a history of immigration, and, whether in terms of successive waves of Inuit inching across the Arctic or woodland tribes pushing into the plains and starting a hunting culture with horses that had escaped from the invading Spaniards in Mexico, change took place through peoples and influences entering to hunt, to raid, to settle, to trade. Horses, pottery, and the agricultural triad of maize, beans and squash, all coming north out of Mesoamerica, had made Canada a place of changing cultures long before Columbus or even Leif Ericson arrived in the Americas.

But Canada remained a receiver of trade and techniques, with no broader or truly political connections, until the end of the fifteenth century, the time when the emergent nation-states of Europe were developing imperialist inclinations and were using new techniques of navigation and warfare to spread their influence and their power. By the late fifteenth century, Bristol and Breton fishermen were on the Grand Banks and in the Gulf of St. Lawrence, and by the sixteenth century, whalers were already penetrating from Europe into the Arctic seas. Beginning with Cabot and Cartier, navigators sponsored by the growing North European maritime powers reached Newfoundland, Acadia and eventually Québec. The French established their bridgeheads at Port Royal and Québec, the English in tiny settlements in Newfoundland, while southward, along the Atlantic coast, the new British settlements followed each other; and not only the French and the English but also the Dutch entered the archipelagos of the Caribbean as rivals of the already established Spaniards; the Scots even tried their luck disastrously in Darien.

Nearly two centuries later, in the late eighteenth century, the southward thrust of the Russians from Alaska and the northward probe of the Spaniards from Mexico would fail to meet because of the bold thrust of British naval power into the Pacific, which led Captain Cook and his ships into Nootka Sound shortly before the Spaniards made their landfall in what is now British Columbia. At the same time, the great Anglo–Scottish fur companies waged their trade war across the northern interior of the continent, which resulted in the victory of the Hudson's Bay Company and the establishment of a City of London sovereignty over Rupert's Land, the very heart of future Canada.

From this point, strategically and commercially, Canada's existence would be dominated for generations by the interests of the reigning world powers, which in the end were to include a home-grown American one—the post-Lincoln United States. Canada would itself be part of a worldwide system, the British Empire, and its very self-definition as a country would be partly dominated by imperial as well as local interests. The desire of British North American colonists in the 1860s to have their own government in form and substance by confederating was paralleled by Westminster's desire to consolidate the imperial frontier with the American republic. And so the work of the surveyors who eventually plotted the Forty-ninth Parallel as a frontier supplemented—as Donald Creighton rightly insisted in books like *The Commercial Empire of the St. Lawrence*—the westward thrust of the fur trade, which the building of the CPR completed by binding the whole structure with steel.

Canada thus entered the company of nations as both economically and politically a member of the surviving imperial group in the Americas, those of Spain and France having disintegrated and the American conversion to imperialism having barely begun. But breakup followed breakup; by the time Canada began to develop truly national ambitions during World War Two, the British Empire was also passing out of existence following the liberation of India in 1947; and Canadian politicians did not feel themselves strong enough to resist the domination of one of the two great imperial agglomerations, that overshadowed by the United States. Priding ourselves on being members of a winning combination in World War Two, we entered into military alliances like The North Atlantic Treaty Organization (NATO) and the North American Air Defence Command, usually called NORAD, in which we had neither independence nor influence, with the same zeal as we have recently shown in entering economic combinations more harmful than useful to us.

The old image of Mahomet's coffin suspended between two magnetic points in Mecca would apply to many countries in the twentieth-century world, Canada among them. But the points of attraction have constantly changed. Before World War Two, Canada seemed part of a sub-world bordering the Atlantic on north and east, the pull of Britain equalling that of the United States, and the Caribbean still serving as a kind of southern anchor. When the Cold War began, the pattern changed: the influence of Britain steadily receded, and Russia challenged us across the Arctic seas, whereas the famous Pacific Rim, with its economically active East Asian nations, became important.

II

TODAY WE ARE GOING THROUGH ANOTHER STAGE in the dissolution of alliances and national relationships, with the collapse of the Warsaw Pact and the Soviet Union itself, and the consequent changes in alignments everywhere. And now, when the United States is also economically—and therefore politically—less powerful than it would like to appear, there is an urgency for Canada to reconsider its position in the world and how that relates to its internal structure, and to its human and material resources as part of a worldwide pattern.

There are negative as well as positive ways in which this

question can be considered, and most of them are connected to our constitutional debates more closely than most Canadians may have thought, for they involve our attitude toward the sovereignty of our country and to the real meaning of this political condition.

Let me begin the negative aspect with a reminiscence dating back some eighteen or nineteen years. My wife and I were doing some preliminary exploration with a television producer for a film on the village people who lived in traditional tribal style in the interior of mountainous Viti Levu, the largest of the Fijian islands. We were accompanied by a member of one of the high chiefly lines of Fiji, without whose noble presence we would have been ignored or—perhaps worse—sent about our business.

We left our Land Rover and walked onto the platform of large flat stones and turf that stretched before the great thatched *mbure* that served as the chief's palace. Raised up on a terrace, a couple of musicians waited with their slit drums, hands held expectantly, and behind them the old one-eyed chief with his attendants. The drums beat into a frenzied staccato, wood on wood, and the chief's orator stood up with his staff and made a step toward us. "Do you come," he called, "in war or in peace?" I could hear an expectant rustle among the young men standing behind the chief; it was almost as if they were waiting for the throwing of spears and the raising of war clubs. "We come in peace," declared our sponsoring chief as we came forward with our traditional gifts, black tarry stick tobacco and Australian silver dollars. He told who we were and what we did, for South Sea Islands manners prevent a man from explaining himself. As we sat down, *kava*, the sacred drink, was made so that we might drink our brotherhood in the old Fijian way.

In effect, Canadians can only say, "We come in peace!" even within our own country, for the days of English conquering French and white men bullying Native peoples are hopefully over, and all we need now is to clear up the debris of that unfortunate era. We have neither the will nor the means to make war on our own in a modern world, and indeed in the last three imperialist wars, the Boer war, World War One and World War Two, Canada served as a dependent member of the British Empire. More recently Canadian troops have served in American operations, like the Korean War and the Gulf War, which were disguised as United Nations campaigns but were so heavily dominated by American materiel, manpower and command that their international nature was a mere pretence. And in each of the alliances to which it still belongs, such as NATO and NORAD, Canada is a minor and uninfluential member, allowing its land to be used for American military bases and manoeuvres. The only occasion in history when Canadian armed forces acted independently and went to war, was against Canadians trying to defend their land and their rights, the Métis of 1885.

It is in this direction that we should open the first stage of our new affirmative attitude to sovereignty. Since we have no real say in who will press the button that starts a war, we should recognize that all through the Cold War period we were being made dependent on the United States for our safety, and we would make ourselves so once again in the event of Russian—or American—nuclear weaponry falling into the hands of future belligerent governments. Although the wording of any alliances we may sustain doubtless provides for the defence of Canada against nuclear attack, the fact is that American strategists regard Canada—the Arctic and the great plains especially—as an expendable territory. It will be over these fragile environments that American defensive systems may bring down enemy weapons with atomic warheads, whose debris would fall on Canadian towns and villages and farms, polluting Canadian air and water, and setting ablaze forests in a conflagration that would have wholly unpredictable, but certainly disastrous, consequences on agriculture, ranching, wildlife and the very viability of human existence. We cannot defend ourselves from such a threat, and the Americans have neither the will nor the means to offer more than a token defence for us. Our membership in these alliances, however, gives an excuse to attack us, since we appear to outsiders as militarily, economically and culturally part of a homogenous North America.

Our alliances are not merely useless to us; they are positively dangerous. And not merely for the perils in which they place us as the possible objects of attack, but because they also encourage the recklessness of the greater powers and the tendency for nations in the modern world to separate into potentially hostile groups.

III

THESE ARE THE KIND OF FACTS that wise peoples, like the Swiss, the Swedes and the Costa Ricans figure out for themselves, withdrawing into political and military neutrality. The Austrians had neutrality forced upon them by the great powers when wartime occupation troops were withdrawn; Austria's emergence through neutrality out of the great poverty of the immediately postwar years is one of the striking phenomena of the late twentieth century.

Effective neutrality for Canada would mean abandoning

all our useless defensive alliances. It would mean refusing to mine materials that might be used in nuclear warfare, and refusal to sell arms of any kind. It would mean reducing our armed forces to the governor general's bodyguard, a couple of thousand peacekeepers and some fishing patrol vessels, or, perhaps rather better, the transformation of the armed forces into environmental corps, each raised and controlled by one of the regions. This would mean that the army can never again be used for centralist political purposes as it was by Pierre Trudeau during the October crisis of 1970, and by Brian Mulroney during the Oka incident of 1990. And, since the cost of equipping men for peaceful activities is so much less than that of equipping them for killing and destroying, taxes could be immediately reduced or the money turned to humanitarian ends. No more high-priced chatter about nuclear submarines! No more vast expenditures on supersonic aircraft that seem to kill only their crews! But real progress in protecting and recovering our environment! Real programs to help the poor peoples of the world help themselves! And a start at buying back our resources and industries from the transnational corporations.

It is only when we have proceeded on this affirmation of our sovereignty that we can develop the second recognition, which is that sovereignty implies also custodianship, and the larger and wealthier the country in natural resources, the greater the custodial responsibility. Given the demise of the Russian empire as we have known it since the days of the tsars, Canada has become the largest land mass in the world, with the planet's largest area of fresh water—rivers and lakes and vast wetlands—enclosed within its frontiers, vast areas of forest, including the rain forests of the Pacific coast, and still, though they are much diminished, some of the most important fish stocks in the world's oceans. Some of the largest flights of migratory wildfowl cross Canadian territory, and they fly over some of the globe's finest terrains for winter sports and summer mountaineering. Much of Canada is indeed barren tundra or land for growing forests rather than crops or pasture, but there are still many square miles of good land, once cultivated, since let go because their size or shape does not fit in with contemporary extensive methods of farming. Such neglected land, abandoned to scrub, is found particularly often in British Columbia and the Maritimes.

This, however we may neglect it, is the land we hold in trust for the world's population. In any true global morality, there is no such thing as absolute possession. Even the first peoples do not have that right, and in their traditions they acknowledge this. Property is a European concept alien to all Native traditions. For them, possession has always been based on usufruct rather than on ownership. One harvests the land's product to the extent of one's need, and one provides for those who also need but cannot harvest.

It was a failure to understand this difference in perceptions of property that led to most of the misunderstanding between first peoples and the latecoming French and English. Often chiefs or bands assigned land to white men on the assumption that they were only granting its use, and then found that in the law of the conquerors they had granted possession. A kind of clumsy compromise with the ancient ways has been reached in the forests, which are now leased rather than transferred to the logging companies. But the leases are generally too long, and the terms usually allow—for derisory stumpage fees—forms of exploitation that transform the land without prospect of natural recovery for generations, or even centuries to come, if not forever. In such ways is the heritage of born Canadians (Native and latercomers alike) being stolen from them; so are the habitats of the creatures with whom we share this terrain, including the wildfowl that include our wet lands in their global peregrinations. What may be irreparable damage is being done to the earth by atmospheric changes caused by things done to rain forests under our control, where the fall of a single giant Sitka spruce can contribute to alterations in the weather patterns of a continent and hence of the whole earth.

The world has grown too small, and its ecological interconnections have been too clearly demonstrated for absolute property to be any more acceptable than absolute rule; if our freedom depends on our respect and love for each other, so the welfare of the planet and all earthly life depends on our willingness to treat its goods with respect, without selfishness. Complex natural circumstances, together with the accidents of political history, have resulted in some countries being richly endowed with natural resources, while other more populous lands are deprived of them. But since conservation means something much broader than consumption, and since a rain forest provides so much more than merely lumber, our great problem is not that of sharing out the products of natural resources where they are needed; it also means making sure the resources are properly used, to provide for renewability where possible, to monitor and, where necessary, counter the effects of exploitation on climate and environment.

It is here that the "have" countries, of which Canada is most assuredly one, must revive their views of possession, and regard it as a matter of generally beneficial usufruct rather than of total ownership. We hold our resources in trust, and the New Testament parable of the talents is not wrongly interpreted if we take it to mean that we shall somehow be called to account for our stewardship. In the world as we know it, the Will of God, or the Mandate of Heaven, or whatever else you may choose to call it, finds expression in the natural consequences of our actions: we clearcut and forests disappear, the climate changes, the vegetation changes, the fish stocks diminish as the bison did. There undoubtedly is a condition of chaos in nature, and no two similar sets of circumstances work out in identically the same way, but the general pattern of cause and effect usually works. We plunder the earth in certain ways and someone or something suffers.

More and more we are entering the "love one another or die" situation. And when we have asserted our sovereignty in the face of the negations of war making, we shall be called to adapt it in the name of peace. Even the traditions to justify this are present in our own societies. The Eskimo hunter gave away the best products of his chase to those who were themselves unable to hunt. Gabriel Dumont, the great Métis leader, would personally assist the old and the disabled by hunting bison especially for them. The barn raising and land clearing bees of the pioneers were occasions when a district's people gave freely of their labour and that of their draft animals to establish the farms of those who could not pay for labour. It was mutual aid at its best, with everyone benefitting from the goodwill of others, without which none could have survived, let alone prospered. The metaphorical bison now are the resources that, without excessively depleting them, we must offer to those whose need is greatest, and the metaphorical barns are all the techniques and materials we can offer to other countries who cannot afford to pay for help at crucial turning points in their economic development.

Here is where our sovereignty must expand, rather than loosen. We take responsibility within the world, and in the process relax our claims to possession so that environmental matters are managed for the good of all the planet's inhabitants, not merely Canadians and not merely humankind.

This implies an entirely new shape of national relations, with collective pride dissolving away on all sides, an entirely new kind of accord making, an entirely new style and substance of diplomacy where, as within the nation, the search for consensus must replace the practice of adversarialism. Lands like Canada and the countries of the Amazon basin, whose environmental policies may affect the whole world through the depletion of natural resources, must be willing to share their heritage responsibly, but the same conversely applies to the great industrial powers. They too must be induced by example, argument, shaming and final agreement, to end their assault on the planet's vital essences, its air and its water. Canada falls into both categories. The needs for changes in its foreign policies are urgent, fundamental and demanding of deep consideration at this moment of constitutional change, when we are considering the social–political shape of our society for the next generation. For it is a different kind of country from the nation-state that those needs demand, a confederation open and flexible and interpenetrating in every direction.

The image that comes to my mind is a homely one, that of an extremely useful piece of kitchen ware, the colander: open for fluid passage, adapted for retaining the essential and letting the unessential go, and yet firm in outline and excellently suited for its purpose.

8

WAYS AND MEANS: THE NECESSARY DISOBEDIENCE

AS I COME TO THESE FINAL PAGES of my book, I realize that what I have been envisaging is something more than an institution, something more real and all-embracing than any constitutional scheme that has yet been proposed. By the time these words have reached print, it is possible that some kind of document called a constitution will have been cobbled together, the sooner the worse. For if it is shaped by federal and provincial political leaders and pushed through their respective parliamentary bodies, the new constitution will be regarded from the outset and later with manifest discontent by most of the people, who ever since the fiasco of Meech Lake have been increasingly conscious of their own disempowerment as citizens.

Yet, at the same time, the alternative ways in which the people can intervene in their future fate are limited by the complexity of the issues involved. A referendum almost always involves a Yes/No answer to a simply stated (but not necessarily uncomplex) question. But there are few questions relating to Canada's future that can honestly be stated with simplicity. Broader in its scope than a referendum, and undoubtedly more sensitive to the complexity of the issues, would be the grand jury, drawn by lot from good women and true men (or vice versa), which we might call a constituent assembly. Party divisions would not be permitted; neither would the presence of professional politicians; but people from all regions and traditions would come together to frame the new social contract.

Here perhaps I have come to the definition we have needed all along, for if we are to attend to all the necessary matters involved in these essays, then a mere constitution will be neither broad nor sensitive enough to embrace them. The social contract, as the Swiss political thinker Jean-Jacques Rousseau expounded it, was partly a myth illustrating how social man emerged from the self-defensive savage solitary (unrevealed of course by paleontologists) of the distant past, and partly a model of how the idyllic conditions of that first contract might be recreated.

Contemporary or slightly later libertarian thinkers, like William Godwin in England and Pierre Joseph Proudhon in France, criticized Rousseau's version of the social contract because of the authoritarian elements in its specifications of rights and duties. They argued that an ossified society, like those envisaged in Plato's *Republic* or More's *Utopia*, would come into being, with human activities circumscribed at all times and in all directions. They equated the rigidities it might produce with those of a benevolent dictatorship, and they were perhaps right in their time, for the great bureaucratic revolutions in eighteenth-century Europe (which included the institutionalization of serfdom and the class system in tsarist Russia) were carried out by autocratic monarchs, among them Frederick the Great of Prussia and Catherine the Great of Russia, who were deeply interested in the writing and thoughts of the French Encyclopedists and their contemporaries, like Rousseau and Voltaire. Certainly the efforts of the Jacobins in 1789–93 to create in France a social contract that would give life to their concepts of freedom, equality and brotherhood, were a tragic failure.

Other critics later condemned the social contract in the same way as they condemned utopian ideas, because they might impose on humanity in the future some pattern related to our imperfect condition. Yet a social contract need not be a rigid legalistic arrangement binding the future to the problems of the present. Where necessary, in agreements dealing with specific issues, it can be explicit in details. But it can also be left open and implicit, a matter of adaptable guidelines, a direction indicated rather than a road laid down. In this way, once its general form is understood, a contract can be expanded and modified as society develops, as the people become more empowered and aware. If the task of developing it were entrusted to a constituent assembly, I would suggest that its members be given two mandates: 1) the drawing up of a constitution that would satisfy immediate demands, like the distinctness of all regional and Native societies, and the granting of Native demands to the extent of what American jurists have called "dependent sovereignty"; and 2) the establishing of the social contract as a continuing goal, under which the roles of politics and politicians dwindle to vanishing points as the nation-state indeed withers away, and the true co-operative commonwealth emerges with the communities, the regions and the confederation playing their proper roles in a world

more open and interpenetrative—united without homogeneity—than has ever existed before.

If we achieve this, the years of argument and disputation
over a new Canada will not have been wasted, as they will
be if all that emerges out of the current constitutional efforts
is merely another revision of the good old BNA. But the
creation of a social contract that will last and change over
the years in time with the people's desire to control their
circumstances more closely, will not be as simple a matter
as posing a vote or offering a referendum on a limited
constitutional package. And here we come to the matter of
Ways and Means.

Central to it is the question of how far and how fast the
people can penetrate the series of screens which politicians
have erected over the centuries, and gain more control over
their lives, their societies, their environments. These are
not merely the screens politicians have created to gain more
control over their world. One is the screen of bureaucratic
procedure, by which whatever may survive of humane understanding in a parliamentary vote is finally denatured by
being interpreted in sets of rules designed to be operated by
impersonal, inhumane and career-oriented bureaucrats.

Inevitably, given the mechanical arrangement of the
public service, there must—and there do—occur points when
decisions of bureaucrats in a capital city, whether Ottawa or
Victoria, Charlottetown or Yellowknife, will go against the
will of small groups whose shared knowledge, based on
experience and awareness of the needs of their locality, can
just as often be aesthetic as economic or political.

If the people are unwilling to accept an official decision
because they believe centrally situated politicians or bureaucrats do not understand their problems, then inevitably the

democratic procedure will broaden into some form of direct action, like old-time juries refusing to find guilt in capital offences. A group of neighbours will encircle a threatened tree to keep power saws away; parents will stop traffic on a dangerous crossing near a school. Indian bands and environmentalists will combine to close off logging roads and prevent the felling of thousand-year-old trees. All such people will be performing what an imperfect system stigmatizes as illegal acts, and following on the 140-year-old insight of Henry David Thoreau, the great American rebel: "As for adopting the ways the state has provided for remedying the evil, I know of no such ways. They take too much time and a man's life will be gone."

It is an old complaint, running back to Hamlet lamenting nearly four hundred years ago "the law's delay. The insolence of office," and to the Greeks two millennia before Hamlet. No democratic system has solved it, perhaps because, as Proudhon used to remark, they were all *systems* and not free arrangements.

Thoreau was not merely the author of that idyll of peaceful and solitary living, *Walden*. He also wrote a tiny essay with enormous influence and consequence over the generations, "On Resistance to Civil Government." Discovered by Gandhi in a prison library in South Africa, a copy of this essay greatly helped the Indian leader in the formulation of his own teaching that bad laws need not be obeyed and how they may be resisted.

Thoreau's ghost hovered over the creation of a free India, and over the success of the great civil rights movement in the United States after World War Two. And perhaps we may even evoke his spirit when speculating about the future of Canada, which he once visited, remarking that given the system he saw prevailing there, "I saw that I would be a bad citizen, that any man who thought for himself and was only reasonably independent would be a rebel."

In taking Thoreau's challenge, as we must when we consider the *ways and means* of changing Canada, we have to consider the tactics and strategies appropriate to those who wish to empower the Canadian people and relate politics to true social and environmental reality. Inevitably, we come to the point of civil disobedience, which more than once has changed the attitudes and the destinies of nations.

When I first proposed this book, my publisher replied to my proposal to discuss civil disobedience that this seemed hardly appropriate in a situation that hopefully would be solved in a legal and constitutional way, the institutions of the old constitution preparing the way for the new one. I am still convinced that, especially when we conceive a constitution expanded and extended into the open form of an evolving social contract, civil disobedience emerges as a necessary extension of ways and means, to be used when political procedures are too slow or the law is, in the words of the ineffable Mr. Bumble, "an ass—an idiot." More precisely, the law is "an old fool," dealing with rules that lack precision in the modern world because they are the products of the common law evolved when England was freeing itself from the arbitrary rule of the kings in the late middle ages. Of such character are the very general provisions against "obstruction" and "public nuisance," often evoked because it is easier for the police to do that than to find a specific law, or the lawyers to create one.

Civil disobedience has been with us at least since the day when the plebians of Rome marched out of their city until their rights were recognized. It is humanity going outside the legal codes and discovering the realities of natural and communal law. It involves the choice to respect or disrespect the law as created by politicians or political bodies. The majority does not enter into this situation; morality does, and the moral man who practises civil disobedience when the laws offend him is usually triumphant in the end.

The man who practises civil disobedience is often regarded as a criminal; the courts condemn him and the prisons receive him. But his criminality is always provisional. It depends on the relativity of so many laws to changing social attitudes. Most of India's leading figures after its liberation in 1947 were convicts under the British rule. Here in Canada, we have witnessed such ironical situations as those offered by Native activists and environmentalists arrested for blocking the roads to loggers in an area later defined as a national park where logging itself became a criminal activity.

The chief characteristic of the civil disobeyer is his willingness to suffer uncivil oppression, to accept for his beliefs beating and imprisonment, torture and death. His weapons are sharp and subtle, those of example and shame. Time and again Gandhi—who was often imprisoned for it—led his satyagrahis in peaceful actions against the British rulers of India; the white-clad ranks marched with perfect discipline to be clubbed down by the police, always forcing the rulers of the Raj over the edge into brutality, until, in the end, the Raj negotiated its own departure with the very men it had imprisoned.

Only recently, the peoples of eastern Europe—of Germany, Czechoslovakia, Poland, Hungary and finally Russia itself—performed some of history's great acts of civil disobedience by surging out in their millions into their ancient streets, men and women, old and young, and shouting their rejection of regimes that quickly fell.

I am not sure whether the recognition of civil disobedience has any place in the making of a constitution, which more and more appears to be an irrelevant political exercise; civil disobedience does have a clear place in a social contract, since, from John Hampden defying tax without representation in seventeenth-century England, and humane juries defying hanging judges in the eighteenth century, it has played its part in the evolution of our ideas of justice in relation to law. It has been a necessary tactic of democratic evolution, and it is linked closely to the idea of the empowerment of the people, a concept that draws little comfort from the political shifts that dominate constitution making. My own feeling is that, if we do end up with a new constitution, we shall soon be virtually ignoring that inadequate political exercise, as we have so largely done in the past, and shall move, as in so many ways we have begun to do, toward a social contract.

And here is where the role of the civil disobeyer comes in. How can we protect the rights and achievements of such moral women and men? The area between law and natural justice is a perilous one, but I suggest that society has far more to gain by tolerating the disobedience of the virtuous and listening to their views, than by shoving them into paddy wagons and imprisoning them as public nuisances.

The problem with civil disobedience lies less with the disobeyer than with vested political and economic interests. The problem cannot be solved, as we try to do now, by relying on generalized laws of obstruction, public nuisance etc., that neither relate to special cases nor take into account those who provoke civil disobedience. If entrepreneurs and power brokers are to remain free in their socially negative activities, so must those who reject and oppose them. Some law of legitimate practical opposition, some code of disobedience and its permissibility, is needed as part of any working social contract. It must recognize that there are more interests involved than those of the nominal property owners, for example Native peoples and environment groups, as well as the lessees of the forest lands. Human rights of recreational enjoyment and animal rights must be recognized, as well as the earth's own right not to be impoverished or irremediably scarred. If they are so recognized, most of the acts of civil disobeyers will cease to be crimes.

There is no question here of legitimizing political violence. Nonviolent action is in any case more effective as well as more moral. Indeed, if violence enters at all into our considerations, it should take the form of a resolution to decrease progressively the violence of humans against other animals. For our own growing liberation should lead toward the liberation of other beings. In this way our social contract will be complete and the "peaceable kingdom" of which I wrote so ironically in the early pages of this book may become a real possibility.